PIUS XII
and the THIRD REICH

Saul Friedländer

PIUS XII
and the
THIRD REICH
A Documentation

Translated from the French and German

by Charles Fullman

New York: Alfred · A · Knopf · 1966

THIS IS A BORZOI BOOK

PUBLISHED BY ALFRED A. KNOPF, INC.

TO THE MEMORY OF MY PARENTS

KILLED AT AUSCHWITZ

Rome (851), 4 via Giovanni Prati
March 4, 1965

Dear Sir:

I regret having kept you waiting so long for an acknowledgment of receipt of the book you were kind enough to send me. I admired the wealth of your documentation which brought back to mind events I followed so closely, with much sorrow, during the course of the Second World War.

It is well that the whole truth be known. It was very difficult during the war to know exactly what was going on. I often regretted that the office of the Secretary of State never thought to keep the cardinals informed by bulletin. I did the best I could by subscribing to two Swiss dailies, the *Basler Nachrichten* and one of two French-language papers, the *Journal de Genève* or the *Gazette de Lausanne*. I avoided going to France for the entire duration of the war, because I would have had to submit to the military honors guaranteed to cardinals by the German concordat. It was only toward the end of 1944 that I was able to resume contact with the French prelates. I never accepted the Pétain regime, nor the idea of collaboration with Nazi Germany.

Allow me to call to your attention a typographical error on page 155: At the beginning of the next-to-last paragraph it should read: "Monseigneur Sericano."

With gratitude for the way in which you have spoken of me, I beg you to accept my thanks and congratulations, with the assurance of my high regard.

✝*Eugène Card. Tisserant*

Cardinal Tisserant is Dean of the Sacred College of Cardinals
Translated from the French by Sophie Wilkins

Rome (851), 4 via Giovanni Prati. Le 4 mars 1965.

Monsieur,

Je regrette de vous avoir fait attendre aussi longtemps un accusé de réception pour le livre que vous avez eu la bonté de m'adresser. J'ai admiré la richesse de votre documentation qui m'a rappelé des évènements suivis de près avec douleur pendant le cours de la deuxième guerre mondiale.

Il est bon que toute la vérité soit connue. Il était très difficile pendant la guerre de savoir exactement ce qui se passait. J'ai regretté plusieurs fois que la Secrétairerie d'Etat n'ait pas songé à renseigner les cardinaux par un bulletin. Je m'arrangeais comme je pouvais en recevant à la fois deux quotidiens suisses, les Basler Nachrichten et un des deux journaux de langue française, Journal de Genève ou Gazette de Lausanne. J'ai évité pendant toute la durée de la guerre d'aller en France car j'aurais dû subir les honneurs militaires que le concordat allemand assurait aux cardinaux. C'est seulement à la fin de 1944 que j'ai pu retrouver le contact avec les prélats francais. Je n'avais jamais admis le régime Pétain ni l'idée d'une collaboration avec l'Allemagne nazie.

Permettez moi de vous signaler à la page 155 une faute d'impression. Il faut lire "Monseigneur Sericano" au début de l'avant-dernier paragraphe.

En vous remerciant pour la manière dont vous avez parlé de moi, je vous prie d'agréer, Monsieur, mes remerciements et mes félicitations avec l'assurance de ma haute considération.

+ Eugène Card. Tisserant

Rome (851), 4 via Giovanni Prati
22 décembre 1965.

Monsieur,

Répondant à votre lettre du 7
décembre, jem'empresse de vous faire savoir que je vous autorise à reproduire ma
lettre du 4 mars 1965.

Veuillez agréer, Monsieur, les
assurances de ma haute considération et
de mon dévouement.

+ Eugène Card. Tisserant

Rome (851), 4 via Giovanni Prati
22 December 1965

Dear Sir:

In reply to your letter of December 7, I hasten
to advise you that you have my permission to reproduce
my letter of March 4, 1965.

Please accept, dear Sir, assurances of my high regard.

✠*Eugène Card. Tisserant*

Author's Foreword to the Present Edition

WHEN THIS BOOK was originally published in France, one of the main arguments brought against it was that the documents presented stemmed from only one source, the German Foreign Office, and were therefore telling only one side of the story. To me, this objection was obvious from the beginning and anyone reading the introduction to the book will note that the provenance of the documents is strongly stressed. However, let me say again that the documents quoted are reports sent by the German ambassadors at the Holy See, or other German diplomatic documents, the truthfulness of which could be checked only if compared with the corresponding documents from the Vatican archives. This book does not at all pretend to be a complete explanation of Pope Pius XII's motives during World War II, but only a contribution to a study of the subject. As such, the German documents seem to me to be of the highest interest.

When preparing this book I attempted several times to get access to the Vatican archives, but in vain. After the publication of the book, many voices arose to ask for a publication of the Vatican counter-documents and the Holy See even mentioned the possibility of publishing a White Book. The Jesuit periodical *Civiltà Cattolica* published two Vatican documents concerning one of the minor events mentioned in this study (a concert supposedly to be given at the Pope's special request in March 1941). These have been the only publica-

tions of Vatican documents up to now. It is my most sincere
wish that these two documents be followed by many others, to
allow a more complete study of this difficult problem. Every
effort has been made to take into account in the present edition
all the pertinent criticisms made about this book so far, and the
new documents just mentioned have been added. I can only
hope that the reader will take this book in the spirit in which
it was written, not as an attempt to draw any final conclusions,
but as a scientific contribution to future research.

July 1965

Just as this book was going to press, the Vatican announced the publication of some of its World War II archives.
The first volume, covering the period from March 1939 to
August 1940, has already been published.[1] This volume, to
be followed by five more, adds interesting details on the
Holy See's policy during that period. However, what has been
published up to now does not, on the whole, seem to con-
tradict in any way the impression given by the documents
published in my book, for the same period.

December 1965

---

[1] *Actes et Documents du Saint-Siège relatifs à la Seconde Guerre
Mondiale. Vol. I: Le Saint-Siège et la Guerre en Europe, mars 1939-
août 1940*. Rome: Libreria Editrice Vaticana; 1965.

CONTENTS

[xi]

CONTENTS

INTRODUCTION

THE ATTITUDE of Pope Pius XII toward the Third Reich and the reasons for his silence in the face of the systematic extermination of the European Jews form the subject of agonizing questions and passionate polemics. Confronted with such a problem, the historian has difficulty in claiming perfect objectivity. Nevertheless, despite the confusion created in people's minds by the very great diversity—and sometimes the strangest —of accusations and refutations, one possibility of honest investigation remains: to adhere, as far as possible, *to the documents*. That is the rule governing the study I have undertaken.

A large proportion of the documents quoted is unpublished; others are known only to a very limited number of specialists; lastly, certain of them have been mentioned in recently published studies,[1] but seldom quoted in full. Now —and this is the second methodological principle here applied —*only quotation of the document in extenso* permits the

---

[1] Jacques Nobécourt: *Le Vicaire et l'Histoire* (Paris: Editions du Seuil; 1964) and Guenter Lewy: *The Catholic Church and Nazi Germany* (New York: McGraw-Hill; 1964). Since the French edition of this book was published, another important book on the subject has appeared: Carlo Falconi: *Il Silencio di Pio XII* (Milan: Sugar; 1965), based on an extensive study of Polish and Yugoslav archives. Dieter Albrecht's *Der Notenwechsel zwischen dem Heiligen Stuhl und der deutschen Reichsregierung* (Mainz: Matthias Grünewald Verlag; 1965), a collection of official notes exchanged between the Holy See and the German Government, covers only the period from October 1933 to March 1937.

reader to evaluate its scope and real shades of meaning. In the majority of cases, therefore, I have avoided making cuts in the documents quoted, even when the style is prolix or when some passages appear tedious. Only passages totally unconnected with the subject, administrative references, polite phrases, and certain repetitions have been omitted.

The documents cited have been restored to their historical context by providing brief notes designed to recall the events of the moment, and occasional added comments, either to assess the probable veracity of the document or to cast light on the facts mentioned. Occasionally, I take a position. In such cases the reader can reject my observation. The text of the document stands.

For the purposes of this study, I have had recourse to published collections of British and American diplomatic documents, to some texts published by the Vatican, to certain unpublished documents of the World Jewish Congress and of the Zionist Archives in Jerusalem, to an unpublished document from Hitler's Chancellery, but chiefly to documents, for the most part unpublished, of the Ministry of Foreign Affairs of the Third Reich.

At the end of World War II, the Allies seized the archives of most of the civilian and military services of the Third Reich which had not been destroyed by the Germans themselves or in the course of bombardments and combat. A large part of the Wilhelmstrasse archives fell into the hands of the Anglo-American forces. Though the files of Minister Joachim von Ribbentrop's office had been almost entirely destroyed, those of the State Secretary's office as well as those of certain important departments of the Ministry were more or less intact, with the exception of files covering the last months of the war. These documents were transported to Washington and

London and microfilmed by the British and the Americans; then, after a certain number of years, they were restored to the Federal Republic of Germany. Today, they are at the disposal of researchers in the German Federal Ministry of Foreign Affairs. A certain number of these documents have been—and are still being—published by a committee of specialists. Up to now, these publications—which, at best, can only include an infinitesimal part of the existing material—relate only to events prior to the date of the German attack on Russia in June 1941.

I have utilized the collection of published German documents and above all, as already indicated, the as yet unpublished files stored at the Ministry of Foreign Affairs in Bonn. Of the latter, the archives of the State Secretary's office dealing with Vatican affairs are by far the most important (Staatssekretär: Vatikan).

The State Secretary's archives concerning Italian affairs (Staatssekretär: Italien), as well as those of the department responsible for relations with the Security Services, particularly as they affect Jewish affairs in Italy (Inland II A B: Juden in Italien) and Vatican affairs (Inland II g: Heiliger Stuhl) supplied some important texts. Lastly, the files of the Department handling liaison with the Armed Forces (Pol I M) have likewise been used.

A study of the policy of the Holy See toward the Third Reich during World War II, based essentially on German diplomatic documents, cannot but be very biased; it goes without saying that no definite conclusions can be drawn without knowledge of the Vatican documents.

Diplomatic reports are often influenced by a desire on the part of their authors to cover themselves vis-à-vis the governments they serve. Consequently, it is only by comparing reports on the same event from the greatest variety of sources that one succeeds, sometimes, in obtaining an objective picture. Unhappily this cannot be done in the case of the present study.

As regards the diplomats of the Third Reich, the difficulty is even greater because it is necessary to take into account all the fears and all the reticences, as well as outbursts of fanaticism, on the part of the servants of a totalitarian regime.

Lastly, the study of questions affecting the Vatican poses, in itself, a special problem. The fact is the Holy See often conceals its opposition to the projects of a government under a semblance of surface amiability which may be deceptive.

In spite of all these difficulties, it seems to me that the German documents can contribute, to a certain degree, to an understanding of the events, and this for three basic reasons: the personalities of their authors; the agreement (on the main issues) among a large number of texts drafted by several diplomats over a period of several years; and the fact that the German documents and diplomatic and other documents, drawn from various sources (chiefly British and American), are in accord regarding certain definite events.

Let us examine these three criteria more closely, and consider first the personalities of Bergen and Weizsäcker, the principal authors of the texts at our disposal.

Little testimony is available concerning the personality of Diego von Bergen, who was the German Ambassador to the Holy See from 1920 to 1943. I should like, however, to call attention to a document from the Reich Ministry for Religious Affairs, written in 1937. In a note to the Wilhelmstrasse, Muhs, State Secretary in the Ministry for Religious Affairs, wrote:

"To my great regret, I am obliged to reiterate the opinion I already have expressed on various occasions that the National-Socialist German Reich today is not being represented at the Holy See with the firmness, clarity of purpose, and zeal necessary in such far-reaching negotiations on church policy."[2]

The telegrams from Ambassador Bergen substantiate the "criticism" of Muhs: the Ambassador was a career diplomat, perfectly familiar with the problems of the Vatican, where he had been serving for many years, and apparently unamenable to the Nazi mystique; none of the terms from the phraseology of the loyal National Socialist would ever be found in his reports. True, his dispatches, like those of all the diplomats of his type who remained in Hitler's service, would be prudently worded whenever they took account of facts at which the Reich leaders might take umbrage. On the whole, however, there is no reason to believe that Bergen's reports were embellished to the point of totally falsifying the information transmitted to Berlin.

Finally, it is not without point to stress that, by reason of the very long period that he spent at the Vatican, Bergen was able to establish with the various members of the Curia—and particularly with Pacelli, the Secretary of State who, in March 1939, was to become Pope Pius XII—a footing of trust which would enable him to gather much confidential information.[3] The private letter which Bergen addressed to State Secretary Ernst von Weizsäcker when his departure from the Vatican was announced in April 1943 clearly indicated the confidence reposed in him by the Curia and above all by the Pope. The objection can obviously be made that Bergen put terms of his own invention into the mouth of Luigi Maglione, the Cardinal Secretary of State, but this would seem most

[2] Note by Muhs, Aug. 6, 1937, *Documents on German Foreign Policy*, Series D (hereinafter referred to as *DGFP*), Vol. I, p. 997.
[3] After his election, Pius XII reminded Bergen of their "friendly relations over a period of nearly thirty years." Cf. p. 24.

[xix]

unlikely. Here, then, is what the Ambassador wrote on April 6, 1943:

¶ The request for an *agrément* (for my successor) hit Maglione like a thunderbolt. There were emotional scenes which I need not describe here. What he said essentially was this: he was utterly surprised and upset. The Curia had quite definitely counted on my remaining in Rome until the end of the war. My particularly close relations with all the leading personalities and, above all, the Pope's quite exceptional attitude toward me made possible, at all times, frank, friendly, informal conversations on even the most delicate questions, such as would be inconceivable with other foreign representatives. This had also been a reason for hoping that it might be possible at the end of the war to bring about an exchange of ideas on a purely friendly and discreet footing, at first, as to the most suitable approach for achieving a settlement of the highly complex questions left pending. Was all this, then, to come to nothing? A change of Ambassador at this moment was, in his view, really impossible![4]

Bergen reassured Cardinal Maglione concerning the personality of his successor, State Secretary Weizsäcker himself. How are we to assess the role of the latter in the context of this study?

Ernst von Weizsäcker's personality is infinitely better known than Bergen's. During the period that concerns us, he was at first State Secretary at the Ministry of Foreign Affairs (the most important personage, therefore, after Minister Ribbentrop) and subsequently, from July 1943 onward, Ambassador to the Holy See. As State Secretary, he bore the main

[4] Letter from Bergen to Weizsäcker, April 6, 1943, Staatssekretär: Vatikan, Auswärtiges Amt, Bonn, Manuskript (hereinafter referred to as: Sts: V, AA, Bonn (MS)).

responsibility for contacts with the Apostolic Nuncio, Msgr. Cesare Orsenigo.

Much has been written on the subject of Weizsäcker, and opinions about his personality differ. On one point, however, most historians are in agreement: in his heart of hearts, Weizsäcker was hostile to the National Socialist regime and he was involved at various times in plans of the German resistance directed against Hitler. Erich Kordt, one of the most active members of the opposition to the regime inside the Ministry of Foreign Affairs itself, describes him in his memoirs in terms imbued with both sympathy and deference: "Among the officials," writes Kordt in particular, "Weizsäcker was not specially popular, but he enjoyed the respect and confidence even of the majority of those not closely associated with him."[5]

Judging from his attitude toward the regime, Weizsäcker, like Bergen, was not a man to invent good news in order to please Ribbentrop and Hitler. In fact, in Weizsäcker's case, there were many occasions when he could be observed doing the opposite. Disturbed as he was by the adventurous policies of the Reich leaders, he sometimes tried to check their ardor by deliberately sending them pessimistic news. Certain telegrams reproduced in Chapter VI of this study convey the impression that at times Bergen used a similar method.

The reluctance of Bergen and Weizsäcker to transmit information erring on the side of optimism, their tendency to dampen the ardor of the Nazi leaders by dwelling, from time to time, on the unfavorable character of the news they were conveying, suggest that where these two diplomats reported particularly welcome information on the attitude of the Sovereign

[5] Erich Kordt: *Nicht aus den Akten* (Stuttgart: Union Deutsche Verlagsgesellschaft; 1950), pp. 179 f.

Pontiff, of the Curia or of the Nuncio in Berlin toward the Reich, the information tended to be accurate.

Very little is known on the subject of Fritz Menshausen, the Counselor of the German Embassy to the Holy See. In contrast, the conduct of Ernst Woermann, Director of the Political Department of the Wilhelmstrasse, was examined in the course of the Wilhelmstrasse trial in 1948: he, too, belonged to the group of officials in the Ministry for Foreign Affairs who were never fervent adherents of National Socialism. In any event, the reports by Menshausen and Woermann, taken as a whole, are of only secondary importance in the context of this study.

The second criterion which seems to lend a certain value to the German documents quoted in the study lies in the fact that the texts are in accord on important problems, and in the permanent character of the data given. For about four years, diplomats of the Reich and agents of the German Secret Services were engaged in a dialogue with the Sovereign Pontiff, with important members of the Curia and with various dignitaries of the Church in different countries; on essential problems, viewed as a whole, those reports are in agreement, the contradictions almost nonexistent.

Lastly—and this constitutes my third criterion of authenticity—there is agreement on the subject of specific events between the German texts and, for example, British or American documentary sources. Attention is drawn, in the first chapter of this study, to the remarkable agreement between the German and British documents and the memoirs of Polish statesmen concerning the attitude of the Holy See during the Polish crisis in the period March–September 1939.

To sum up, I repeat that so long as the German documents cannot be compared with corresponding texts in the Vatican

Archives, any exposition of the facts shows only one aspect of affairs and, perhaps, of men. Nevertheless, with due regard to the various criteria just examined, it can be maintained that the German documents, and the picture of the situation they give, have an undeniable historical value, though it will be our duty to treat them with all necessary caution and reserve. The commentaries will tend to pose questions rather than make assertions.

The study, as its title indicates, aims essentially at illuminating the attitude of Pope Pius XII toward the Third Reich. I have subjected myself to strict limitations of time: March 1939, the date of the Pope's election, marks the beginning of my researches; September 1944, the date when my documentary sources dry up, marks their end. For that brief period of five years, I shall train my beam on the Pope, on his close collaborators, and on his opposite numbers, the leaders of the Third Reich, in their relations with the Holy See.

Is such a limitation of subject matter acceptable? Can one understand the attitude of Pius XII without having made a detailed study of his earlier career, at least from 1917, when he was appointed Nuncio in Munich, until his elevation to the Supreme Pontificate? Can the motives for certain of his decisions be grasped without analysis of the general situation of the Church and, in particular, the situation of the Church in Germany and its relations with National Socialism?

My choice, it seems to me, is justified for two reasons. On the one hand, in commenting on the texts presented, I shall indicate as briefly as possible, while endeavoring to convey essentials, the general data required for an understanding of the document, referring sometimes to the period before 1939 and often to the situation of the Church during the war. On the other hand, the recent works of Messrs. Nobécourt and Lewy are particularly illuminating, the first about "the apprentice years of Dom Eugenio Pacelli," and the second on the subject of the relations between the Church in Germany and National Socialism. Both describe in detail the relationship between the Holy See and the Third Reich during the tenure of Pius XII. In dealing with matters already so well studied, I have thought it superfluous to go over the ground again at length.

By contrast, these two authors gave rather brief treatment to the problem which forms the real subject of this work (M. Nobécourt certainly devoted some remarkable pages to it, but he did not have access to documents in the German archives; as for Mr. Lewy, he concentrated the main weight of his researches on the policy of the Church in Germany and, although he had opportunity to utilize the archives of the Reich Ministry for Foreign Affairs, he scarcely made use of them at all for the purpose of analyzing the attitude of Pius XII during the war years).

Another argument—more serious, perhaps, than the preceding one—will be leveled against the method of investigation I have chosen. By its very nature, a diplomatic document describes and analyzes the given data in a decision in terms which are of significance in the political (or military) "game"; the moral implications of an act, the anguish which a grave decision may have caused in the conscience of the person assuming responsibility for it, does not interest the diplomat and occupies his attention only incidentally. For this very reason, diplomatic documents are inadequate sources for the historian who wishes to understand the deeper motives underlying an important decision which rises above the level of a simple maneuver. These observations, which apply to the study of the initiatives of any and every statesman, become patently obvious when we enter the domain of decision of a spiritual leader, who is often moved by considerations of an essentially religious character.

Such are the limits beyond which this investigation may not go. Even as a political personage, Pius XII cannot be studied solely on the basis of the diplomatic documents to which we have had recourse. These texts throw light only on certain aspects of a policy and only on some traits of a personality. However incomplete the image so obtained may be, I hope nevertheless that these documents, presented without prejudice, will make a useful contribution to historical research.

I should like to express gratitude to all those who have lent their assistance: to Simonne and Jean Lacouture, as well as to Jacques Nobécourt whose counsel and comments have been extremely valuable. It must be pointed out, however, that although I have taken into account a large number of suggestions, I bear sole responsibility for this text, and it goes without saying that any errors of fact which may have slipped into it, as well as hiatuses in the assessment of events or errors of judgment which the reader may uncover, should be attributed to the author alone.

My thanks go also to Herr Johannes Ullrich of the Ministry for Foreign Affairs, and to Herr Walter Vogel of the Federal Archives, of the Federal Republic of Germany, to Mr. Alexander Bein of the Zionist Archives in Jerusalem, and Mr. Gerhardt Riegner of the World Jewish Congress, for the help which they were kind enough to give me in researching the documents. Finally, I want to express my gratitude to Mme Yvette Surget for her very effective collaboration.

SAUL FRIEDLÄNDER

Geneva, 1964

PIUS XII
and the THIRD REICH

Chapter I

THE INTERNATIONAL CRISIS

March–September 1939

1. The Rapprochement between the Church and the Reich

ON MARCH 2, 1939, Cardinal Eugenio Pacelli, Secretary of State to Pius XI, was elected Pope, and took the name Pius XII. The next day, Counselor Du Moulin, Head of the Department of Vatican Affairs at the Reich Ministry for Foreign Affairs, prepared a memorandum on the political tendencies and the personality of the new Sovereign Pontiff:

¶ *Pope Pius XII (Cardinal Pacelli)*
CAREER:

2. III. 1876	Born in Rome
1917	Nuncio in Munich
	Participated loyally in Vatican proposals regarding mediation for peace
1920–9	Nuncio in Berlin
1929	Cardinal
1930	Cardinal Secretary of State
	Traveled to America and France

Previous Attitude toward Germany

¶ Pacelli was regarded at the outset as very Germanophile. He is well known for his excellent knowledge of the German language. His advocacy of an orthodox Church policy repeatedly brought him into conflict with National Socialism on matters of principle. Nevertheless, it is denied that he had any part in the forceful policies of Pius XI, particularly the markedly hostile speeches of that Pope. On the contrary, he made repeated efforts to achieve compromises and gave expression to his wish for friendly relations with our Embassy.

Previous Attitude toward Italy

¶ Pacelli has always been in favor of good relations with Mussolini and with Fascist Italy. In particular, he encouraged and supported the nationalist posture of the Italian clergy. His brother played a leading part in the conclusion of the Lateran Treaties.

Previous Attitude toward Other Countries

¶ The new Pope has probably adopted no firm political positions. Attempts have been made in French quarters to represent Pacelli's two journeys to France as proof of his Francophile tendencies. Our Embassy on the other hand stressed that the journeys were purely religious in character. Similarly, the trips to America were merely an expression of Vatican world policy . . .

General Characteristics

¶ The picture that emerges from the reports of our Embassy is that of a highly gifted, very industrious and knowledgeable person, far above the average and of vast political ex-

[4]

perience, a man able to accommodate himself dispassionately to the requirements of what seems to him the right policy and who is not averse to compromise. His great personal sensitivity is repeatedly emphasized; this also applies to press attacks, cartoons, and similar things.

Recent criticism, alleging that he had not shown sufficient resistance to the forceful policies of the Pope, was silenced when, on the death of Pius XI, he took over the functions of a Papal Chamberlain and performed them in exemplary fashion. He opposed the pressure of the intransigents with great firmness and, at the same time, came out in favor of understanding and conciliation. It was this attitude that decided the election in his favor.[1]

Thus, it was known in Berlin that the Cardinal who had just been elected Pope was very "Germanophile." It was remembered, no doubt, that the former Nuncio at Munich and Berlin was the initiator of the Concordat between the Holy See and the Third Reich[2] and that, when relations between the Church and the National-Socialist regime became strained, the attitude of the Secretary of State was, according to the telegrams sent by Ambassador Bergen, always more flexible than that of Pius XI.

When the Nazis began, as early as the fall of 1933, to infringe the clauses of the Concordat, it was Msgr. Pacelli who prevented Pius XI from protesting openly.[3] A year later, when the crisis between the Reich and the Church was worsening and the Secretary of State was in Buenos Aires, Bergen, in a

---

[1] Memorandum by Du Moulin, March 3, 1939, StS: V, AA, Bonn (MS).
[2] Guenter Lewy: op. cit., Chap. 3.
[3] Telegram from Bergen to Berlin, Oct. 16, 1933, *DGFP* (C, II), pp. 3 f.

telegram, expressed the fear that without the moderating presence of the Cardinal the Pope might make decisions in regard to Germany which could have disastrous consequences.[4] Some weeks earlier, Msgr. Pacelli had intervened, involuntarily no doubt, to assist the electoral campaign of the Nazis in the Saar, on the eve of a plebiscite which was to decide the future of that region.[5] In spite of the growing difficulties which the Church encountered in Germany from 1936 on, the benevolent attitude of the Cardinal was not denied. In March 1937, the encyclical *Mit brennender Sorge,* an indictment of the neo-pagan theories of National Socialism and of the antireligious measures of the Reich, was published.[6]

Some weeks later, Pius XI publicly supported George William Cardinal Mundelein of Chicago, who had launched an attack of unparalleled violence against Hitler; on the eve of the Pope's address, Bergen was received by Msgr. Pacelli and, on July 23, reported to Berlin the substance of their discussion:

¶ In striking contradiction to the behavior of the Pope, however, are the statements of the Cardinal Secretary of State during the call that I made on him on the 16th, the day before the Pope's discourse. This was the first call after my return, and the conversation was of a private nature. Pacelli received me with decided friendliness and emphatically assured me during the conversation that normal and friendly relations with us would be restored as soon as possible; this applied particularly to him, who had spent 13 years in Germany and had always shown the greatest

---

[4] Telegram from Bergen to Berlin, Oct. 12, 1934, ibid. (C, III), p. 478.
[5] Guenter Lewy: op. cit., p. 188.
[6] It goes without saying that, as Secretary of State, Cardinal Pacelli contributed to the drafting of this Encylical (cf. on this point *L'Osservatore della Domenica,* June 28, 1964).

sympathy for the German people. He would also be prepared at any time for a discussion with outstanding personages such as the Foreign Minister and Minister President Göring. I replied that I hoped the time would come when such a meeting could be arranged [. . .][7] Speaking frankly, I personally consider it impossible at the present time in view of the serious controversy caused by the encyclical, *"Mit brennender Sorge,"* and other events, and in view of the extreme tension. When I mentioned the interpellation (*interpretation*) given his trip to France by the French press (for instance, the *Journal* and the *Humanité*), Pacelli animatedly replied that the trip had been of a purely religious nature and—he could assure me of this most definitely—had served no political purpose; the Vatican had never thought of even an indirect demonstration against Germany, let alone any attempts at encirclement as had been claimed in the *Angriff*. If a religious festival of significance equal to that in Lisieux should some day be arranged in Germany, he would be most happy to go there.[8]

In April 1938, Cardinal Pacelli again had an opportunity to express his goodwill toward Germany when he received Herr Greiser, President of the Danzig Senate, who was passing through Rome. On April 8, State Secretary Ernst von Weizsäcker noted:

¶ Senate President Greiser, on his way back from Rome to Danzig, came to me to add the following supplementary oral remarks to his written report on the subject of his conversation with the Cardinal Secretary of State: Pacelli

---

[7] Occasional gaps in the German telegrams, indicated throughout by bracketed ellipsis as above, represent breaks in the cipher, as received, in which these messages were usually sent. (Translator's note)
[8] Telegram from Bergen to Berlin, July 23, 1937, *DGFP*, Series D, Volume I, pp. 990–2.

had repeatedly conveyed to him in strong terms the need for a settlement between the Vatican and the Reich and had ventured so far as to state that he, Pacelli, was ready to come to Berlin for negotiations, if desired to do so.[9]

In his memorandum of March 3, 1939, Counselor Du Moulin let it be understood, as we have seen, that the conciliatory activity of Cardinal Pacelli during the few weeks between the death of Pius XI on February 9 and the opening of the conclave had assured the ex-Secretary of State his election to the papacy. These remarks are confirmed from a rather good source: on March 2, the very day the new Sovereign Pontiff was elected, Count Galeazzo Ciano, Italy's Minister for Foreign Affairs, noted in his diary that on the previous day Pignatti di Custoza, Italian Ambassador to the Holy See, told him that Pacelli was the candidate favored by the Germans.[1]

On March 2, the Papal Chamberlain became Pius XII. From the moment of his election, he did all that could be done to promote the rapprochement between the Vatican and the Third Reich which he had wanted when he was only Secretary of State.

On March 5, Ambassador Bergen reported the details of his first audience with Pius XII:

¶ In accordance with my request, the Acting Secretary of State had quickly forwarded to the Pope the congratulations of the Führer and Reich Chancellor and those of the Reich

[9] Memorandum by Weizsäcker, April 8, 1938, ibid., p. 1031.
[1] Galeazzo Ciano: *The Ciano Diaries, 1939–1943* (New York: Doubleday; 1946), p. 35. It should be noted, however, that the German press was hostile to Cardinal Pacelli. For a time, there may possibly have been a divergence of view between Goebbels and Ribbentrop regarding the probable attitude of Pius XI's Secretary of State toward the Reich if he were elected Pope.

Government. Yesterday, before the evening was out, the Pope sent word to me that he wished to receive me this morning.

In the course of the audience, during which I expressed our congratulations once again, the Pope emphasized that I was the first Ambassador he had received; he felt it important, he said, to charge me personally with the task of delivering his deeply felt thanks to the Führer and Reich Chancellor; with these, he said, he combined his most sincere wishes for the well-being of the German people whom, having known them for many years during his activity in Munich and Berlin, he had learned to esteem and love more and more. The Pope linked with these words his "ardent wish for peace between Church and State"; he had often expressed this to me as Secretary of State, but today, as Pope, he would like to confirm it explicitly.

As an indication of his attitude toward the various forms of government, he reminded me in the course of the conversation of his address in German to the Eucharistic Congress in Budapest last year. There, as is well known, he expressed himself thus: "It is not the business of the Church to take sides in purely temporal matters and concerns between the various systems and methods that may be considered for mastering urgent problems of the day."

Switching the conversation to the personal plane, the Pope greeted me most cordially, stressing that our friendly relations of nearly thirty years now must continue unchanged in the future.[2]

In his very first interview with Bergen, Pius XII dwelt upon his profound sympathy for Germany which went back

[2] Telegram from Bergen to Berlin, March 5, 1939, *DGFP* (D, IV), p. 598.

to the thirteen years he had spent as Apostolic Nuncio in that country. This statement was often to recur in the years that followed. Moreover, the Sovereign Pontiff let it be clearly understood that the political regime installed by Hitler seemed to him just as acceptable as others.

The Pope, taking the defense of the Church as his first duty, manifestly desired to obtain through maximum conciliation what the firmness of his predecessor had been unable to achieve.

On March 6, Pius XII addressed the following letter to Hitler:

¶ Having been elevated to the papal throne as the result of a statutory poll of the College of Cardinals, We deem it Our duty to inform you, as a Chief of State, of Our election.

At the same time, We desire, from the beginning of Our pontificate, to express the wish to remain united by the bonds of profound and benevolent friendship with the German people, who are entrusted to your care. We call upon Almighty God to bestow upon the German people the true felicity which religion cannot but nourish and increase.

We fondly remember the long years during which We lived in Germany as Apostolic Nuncio and in the course of which We did all in Our power to establish harmonious relations between Church and State, in a spirit of mutual understanding and open-hearted collaboration in the interests of both parties; afterwards, we sought to make satisfactory provision for the implementation of the agreement reached.

Now that the responsibilities of Our pastoral function have increased Our opportunities and strengthened Our purpose, how much more ardently do We wish to reach that goal!

We pray that Our great desire for the prosperity of the

German people and for their progress in every sphere may, with God's help, come to full realization.[3]

As Msgr. Giovanetti, one of the official historians of Pius XII, indicates, this letter "in length and in the sentiments it expresses, differs totally from the other official letters sent by the Vatican at that time."[4]

Both the letter to the Führer and the first conversation between Pius XII and Bergen indicated the nature of the relations which the new Pope wished to restore with the Reich; yet, on March 11, he appointed as Secretary of State, Cardinal Luigi Maglione, who, for several years, had been Nuncio in Paris. In a telegram of the same date, Bergen explained the true significance of this gesture:

¶ Cardinal Luigi Maglione, who has been appointed Secretary of State by the Pope, has been known to me for years through his activity as *Minutante* in the Secretariat of State and as Nuncio in Berne and Paris. He is a personality of high intellectual qualities and adroitness who, I should judge, will not show lack of understanding in his attitude to the new times. He has always gone out of his way to maintain good relations with the Embassy and, in his conversations with me, has made no secret of his friendly feelings for Germany. When he was appointed Nuncio in Paris, the French wanted to refuse him the *agrément* on account of his allegedly pronounced Germanophile outlook. Thanks to his diplomatic skill, he was nevertheless very quickly able to achieve the best possible footing in his relations with influential French personalities. If French press now claims that both he and Pope are particularly pro-French, I am neverthe-

[3] Text quoted by Alberto Giovanetti: *L'Action du Vatican pour la Paix 1939–1940* (Paris: Fleurus; 1963), p. 34.
[4] Ibid.

less convinced that, following the line unmistakably adopted by Pius XII, he will endeavor to bring about a settlement with Germany.

Venture to suggest you recommend friendly restraint on part of press in assessing Maglione.[5]

The judgment made by Bergen about the personality of Cardinal Maglione and his probable political tendencies is not of any particular importance, because a Pope as well informed on political and diplomatic problems as was Pius XII obviously would assume responsibility for making all important decisions and would relegate his Secretary of State to secondary functions.

On March 13, Bergen commented on the letter addressed by the Pope to Hitler:

¶ Letter to the "Führer and Chancellor of the German Reich" from Pius XII announcing his election to the papacy was sent today without formality by the hand of Secretary of Legation Picot owing to lack of time. Its basic attitude is considerably friendlier than was that of Pius XI to the Reich President at that time. . . . Specially worthy of note is fact that this occasion, too, is used for expression of wish for understanding.

Drafting of German text reveals hand of Pope, especially since reliably informed that he has explicitly reserved the handling of German questions for himself.

Pius XII's letter evokes memory of letter addressed to Emperor William I in February 1878 by Leo XIII after his election as successor to the zealot, Pius IX, in which, on the occasion of his enthronement, he expressed regret at finding

[5] Telegram from Bergen to Berlin, March 11, 1939, StS: V, AA, Bonn (MS).

[12]

that the good relations once existing between Prussia and the Holy See no longer prevailed. In the ensuing correspondence, letters countersigned by Bismarck were sent to Leo XIII by Emperor William and by Crown Prince, acting for wounded father after attempt on latter's life. Letters laid heavy emphasis on the independence and interests of the state, but, using conciliatory words, started the gradual process, often interrupted, of putting an end to the *Kulturkampf.*[6]

On March 17, Bergen added further details concerning the significance of the letter from Pius XII to the Führer:

¶ The Pope has intimated to me that the Führer was the first Head of State whom he notified of his election as Pope; he had also broken with the usual protocol when he not only signed, as was customary, the letter drawn up in Latin, but also the German draft, which was not to be considered as a mere translation. He had also wished by these means to intimate his sympathetic attitude to Germany and his desire for peace.

The new Cardinal Secretary of State, Maglione, to whom I paid my first visit only today, received me with marked cordiality. Without going into details he said, in allusion to German-Vatican relations, that I knew his wishes, and that he only hoped they would be realized in the not too distant future, in spite of the existing difficulties of which he was well aware.

L'Osservatore Romano has again received instructions to desist from attacks against the German Government. In effect, reproduction of anti-German press comments has recently been refrained from.

6 Telegram from Bergen to Berlin, March 13, 1939, *DGFP,* Series D, Volume VI, p. 29.

In view of the unmistakably forthcoming attitude of the Curia, I leave it to your discretion whether the press be recommended to continue a restrained objectivity towards Vatican affairs, the more so as this attitude has met with appreciation here, especially in Italian circles also. For the time being there is no question of our taking other measures.[7]

It may be noted that Ambassador Bergen, while underlining the fundamental change in the policy of the Holy See toward the Reich, continued to show restraint. He doubtless knew that Berlin would not take any favorable steps in the realm of religious policy, and certainly not in the campaign against confessional schools. He tried to induce the Minister for Propaganda not to resume the attacks on the Vatican that had been customary in Pius XI's time. In the margin of the telegram, State Secretary von Weizsäcker put down a question to Aschmann, Head of the Press Department of the Ministry of Foreign Affairs: "Amb[assador] Aschmann: Will this suggestion be followed? Weizsäcker 20 (III)." A day later, Aschmann wrote in the margin of the same document: "Hr. Zeileisen: Pl[ease] write to R[eich] Prop[aganda] M[inistry]"; and under this, for Weizsäcker: "St[ate] S[ecretary]: R[eich] Prop[aganda] M[inistry] requested to act accordingly. Aschmann 21 (III)."[8] In point of fact, the attacks on the Pope and the Vatican were soon to disappear from the pages of German newspapers.

On March 15, the Germans occupied Czechoslovakia. On the 22nd, Bergen wrote:

¶ For confidential information. I learn from a well-informed source that urgent attempts have been made, especially on

7 Telegram from Bergen to Berlin, March 17, 1939, ibid.
8 Ibid.

[14]

the French side, to prevail upon the Pope to associate himself with the protests of the democratic States against the annexation of Bohemia and Moravia to the Reich. The Pope has declined these requests very firmly. He has given those around him to understand that he sees no reason to interfere in historic processes in which, from the political point of view, the Church is not interested.[9]

It is possible that a Franco-British démarche was made to the Holy See to persuade the Pope to join the protests of the democracies against the dismemberment of Czechoslovakia by the Reich. There is no trace of it in the memoirs of François Charles-Roux, French Ambassador to the Vatican, or in British diplomatic documents. However, this fact does not detract from the special character of the statements attributed by Bergen to the Sovereign Pontiff. The change which had taken place in the policy of the Holy See toward the Reich, once Pius XI had passed from the scene, was once again made evident: at the time of the annexation of Austria by the Reich, a procedure which many people might have thought normal (for those days), Pius XI had compelled Theodor Cardinal Innitzer, head of the Austrian episcopate (who had ordered the bishops and the local clergy to vote for the *Anschluss*), to issue a public and humiliating retraction. Incidentally, Bergen had commented on that event in a dispatch of April 6, 1938:

¶ As I learned confidentially, the communiqué which is to appear this evening in the *Osservatore Romano* was wrested from Cardinal Innitzer with pressure that can only be termed extortion. Innitzer resisted to the utmost, but was able to effect only a few concessions. In this matter, too, the Pope

[9] Telegram from Bergen to Berlin, March 22, 1939, ibid., p. 74.

had allowed himself to be swayed by his morbid irritation with Germany . . .[1]

The attitude of Pius XII, then, was very different. Nevertheless, the liquidation of Czechoslovakia prompted a complete reversal among the majority of those who were in favor of conciliating the Reich. Again, the policy change effected by the successor to Pius XI came out even more strongly a month later when, after the German troops had marched into Prague, he addressed a group of German pilgrims:

¶ I hear [writes Bergen on April 25] that Pope Pius XII yesterday received in audience some 160 German travelers in Rome. During the audience, he made a short speech in German which, according to Germans and Italians within earshot, contained the following passage:

"We have always loved Germany, where We were privileged to spend years of Our life, and We love it much more now. We rejoice at the greatness of Germany, at her resurgence and her prosperity, and it would be false to maintain that We do not desire a flourishing, great, and strong Germany. But for that very reason We wish, too, that the rights of God and the Church may always be recognized, because the more these rights are guarded and made the basis of constructive effort, the more stable will be the foundation on which greatness is built."

It is further reported to me that the Pope greeted the Germans with particular cordiality and himself joined in the German hymn "Grosser Gott wir Loben Dich," which they struck up.[2]

[1] Telegram from Bergen to Berlin, April 6, 1938, *DGFP* (D, I), p. 1031.
[2] Telegram from Bergen to Berlin, April 25, 1939, StS: V, AA, Bonn (MS).

On May 2, State Secretary von Weizsäcker in his turn noted down information from an Italian source on the policy of Pius XII toward the Reich:

¶ The Italian Ambassador today took up with me information communicated to him by the Reich Minister of Foreign Affairs to the effect that in a recent address the Pope had adopted a more conciliatory attitude toward Germany. Attolico then went on to say that his Government had been told by an Italian informant that the Pope, on assuming office, had forbidden *L'Osservatore Romano* to continue its policy of pinpricks toward both Italy and Germany. The Pope, he said, wished to arrive at a decent *modus vivendi* with Germany, if a deeper understanding was not feasible.

Attolico added further that the Pope, upon assuming office, had written not only the customary official letter, required by protocol, to the German Government, but also a personal letter in German to the Führer, which was intended as a particularly accommodating gesture.[3]

The information concerning the instructions given to *L'Osservatore Romano* seems accurate, because it was not until several weeks after the German attack on Poland that the organ of the Vatican resumed its policy of criticizing the Reich, a policy which, as we shall see, was to give rise to a variety of incidents and which finally came to an end on May 16, 1940, on fresh orders from the Pope. We already know the text of the letter addressed to Hitler by Pius XII. The significance attached to it by Attolico confirmed both what Bergen had written and Msgr. Giovanetti's observations as to its special importance.

[3] Memorandum by Weizsäcker, May 2, 1943, ibid. (MS).

2. *An Attempt at Mediation*

ON APRIL 14, 1939, President Franklin D. Roosevelt sent a message to Hitler and Mussolini asking them to abstain for ten years from any aggression against thirty states designated by name. A few days earlier, Italy had attacked and occupied Albania.

Roosevelt's message was favorably received by the entire world with the exception of the Axis countries and, it seems, the Vatican. On April 21, Ambassador Bergen wrote to the Wilhelmstrasse:

¶ Roosevelt's "Peace Appeal," I hear, is being severely criticized in circles close to the Vatican. Naturally every action in the service of peace is to be welcomed, it is said . . . Roosevelt, on the other hand, has made the mistake of only addressing two specific Heads of Government, and in addition of making public this entirely one-sided appeal. In content, his appeal could on many points be called naive, even childish . . . The proposal for a guarantee contained in the document is also a blunder, it is said, owing to its time limit, as it gives grounds for the suspicion that America intends to use this period of security for going on undisturbed in developing and strengthening her armaments for the event of war.[4]

At the moment when Roosevelt issued his appeal, Pius XII, in turn, was preparing a mediation move in a spirit very

[4] Telegram from Bergen to Berlin, April 21, 1939, *DGFP*, Series D, Volume VI, p. 300. Bergen's report seems confirmed by the attitude of *L'Osservatore Romano*. In an editorial of April 19, the semi-official organ of the Holy See confined itself to reporting press reactions in various countries to Roosevelt's message, devoting considerable space to the hostile reactions in Berlin and Rome and only a few lines to the positive reactions in London and Paris.

different from that of the American President; a negative response on the part of the Pope toward the American plan was, therefore, not outside the realm of possibility. Msgr. Giovanetti reported that Roosevelt had sent, through the medium of the Apostolic Delegate in Washington, a request to the Pope to support his intervention with the governments in Berlin and Rome. Pius XII is said to have conveyed the reply that "in the present state of diplomatic relations with the German Government, a démarche by the Holy See would be inopportune, but that he would not fail to approach the Italian Government."[5] Now Giovanetti, who generally was not loth to quote documents which might bolster his theses, made no mention of any démarche by the Pope to Mussolini. At the beginning of May, on the other hand, Pius XII transmitted proposals of his own to Hitler, which indicates that the argument invoked in the reply to Roosevelt, that diplomatic relations between the Holy See and the Reich were bad, was merely an excuse. On May 4, Cesare Orsenigo, the Apostolic Nuncio in Berlin, was received by the Führer at the Berghof:

¶ The Nuncio informed the Führer that the Pope had instructed him to propose to the Führer a conference of the five Great Powers of Europe to seek a solution to the political questions outstanding. The Pope was deeply concerned about the tension in Europe and wished to do everything that lay in his power to ward off the danger of war from mankind. The purpose of the conference, the form and nature of which he did not specify, would be primarily to find solutions to the two most urgent questions, namely, in the first instance the German-Polish problem and secondly the Franco-Italian problem.

[5] Giovanetti: op. cit., p. 51.

The Führer asked the Nuncio to convey his thanks to the Pope for this suggestion, and opened by saying that he would first of all have to get in touch with Mussolini as he would not do anything without him. His relationship with Mussolini was one of close friendship, based on frankness and loyalty. He and the Duce would at all times act in unison.

The Nuncio agreed to this and said that the Pope would also approach Mussolini at the same time.

Examining the possibility of such a conference the Führer said that he did not actually believe that there was a danger of war as the tension was due more to propaganda than to facts . . .

Long declarations by Hitler on international problems followed, and:

¶ . . . In conclusion the Führer again asked the Nuncio to express his real gratitude to the Holy See. He would get into touch with the Duce immediately and he instructed the Reich Foreign Minister to take the necessary steps at once when he visited Italy. In a very short time he would then let the Pope have his answer.[6]

The Pope's plan, which was to have no concrete results, contained one point of considerable interest. Pius XII addressed himself to the five European Great Powers which, as he saw it, were Italy, Germany, Great Britain, France and Poland. Nothing was said about the Soviet Union. Lord Halifax, Britain's Foreign Minister, pointed out this fact to Msgr. Godfrey, the Apostolic Delegate:

[6] Memorandum by Walter Hewel, May 10, 1939, *DGFP* (D, VI), pp. 426 f.

¶ . . . I added that there would also be many who would regret the omission of Russia from the list of Powers to which his Holiness was making an approach. His Grace (the Apostolic Delegate) replied, as I anticipated, that in no circumstances would it be possible for the Pope to consider such an approach . . .[7]

Msgr. Godfrey's categorical reply accurately reflected the attitude of the Pope. Hostility toward Bolshevism and the Soviet Union was the determining factor in numerous political decisions made by Msgr. Pacelli when he was merely Secretary of State; it was to have a decisive influence on the policy of Pius XII during the war. Atheistic Communism had been solemnly condemned by Pius XI in his encyclical *Divini Redemptoris* of March 1937, five days after his condemnation of the neopagan theories of National Socialism; but, while the latter had been denounced only in relatively moderate terms, the condemnation of the Communist regime was categorical and irreversible.

To the doctrinal foundations laid down by Pius XI, his successor added a personal aversion to Communism which dated from the time of his "contacts" with the Bavarian Soviets in 1919. In 1921, he described them to a correspondent of *Le Matin*:

¶ I was one of the few non-German eyewitnesses of the Bolshevik regime which ruled in Munich in April 1919. There were actual Russians at the head of that Soviet Government; any ideas of right, liberty and democracy were suppressed; the Soviet press was the only press allowed. The Nuncio's residence itself was riddled with bullets in the

[7] Telegram from Halifax to Osborne, May 5, 1939, *Documents on British Foreign Policy*, Third Series, Vol. V, pp. 435 f. (hereinafter referred to as *DBFP*).

fighting between the Communists and the troops of the Republican Government. Armed Spartacists forced their way into the residence and, as I protested vigorously against this violation of international law, one of them threatened me with his revolver. I know the odious conditions in which hostages were massacred.[8]

It is clear, then, that Pius XII was not inclined to invite the Soviet Union to a conference in arranging which the Holy See took the initiative. Furthermore, it is possible that, in excluding Moscow from the meeting envisaged, the Sovereign Pontiff was pursuing an immediate diplomatic goal: in April 1939, negotiations had begun between the Western Powers and the Soviet Union with a view to the eventual signing of a defense pact; they were not kept as secret as the first contacts between Berlin and Moscow. The Holy See could not look with favor on a return of the Soviet Union to the European scene, from which it had been excluded by the Munich Accords. A conference to which the Russians were not invited might thrust them back into the isolation which they were on the point of smashing.

But all these are nothing more than hypotheses. Pius XII seemed, above all, to be seeking a means of safeguarding the peace. His plan failed.

On June 8, Bergen was received by the Pope in private audience. Next day, he wrote to Ribbentrop:

¶ Dear Herr Reich Minister:
The private audience granted to my wife and myself yesterday—at which by my request I was first received alone—gave me the opportunity to speak in accordance with your instructions.[9] The Pope was so interested, and so delighted,

[8] Quoted by Nobécourt: op. cit., p. 136.
[9] These could not be found.

at the possibility of paving the way for friendly relations between us and the Curia, that he prolonged our conversation again and again, and kept the Spanish Minister, Serrano Suñer, and the delegation of Spanish legionaries waiting for more than half an hour.

The conversation touched on this and that. I spoke on the following lines: The Pope's pronouncements, various gestures, the conveyance of his congratulations on the occasion of the Führer's fiftieth birthday, the address to German pilgrims of which you are informed, etc., had given us the impression and aroused the hope that a new epoch had dawned for German-Vatican relations. In your view it was quite possible for Church and State to dwell peacefully together within the same confines. Should the Vatican's endeavors be thus directed, you would be favorably disposed towards them. In response to your request for proposals, I had characterized as of prime importance the elimination of the present mutual mistrust and the gradual creation of confidence. The *détente,* which was already perceptible, would have to be promoted and a press truce could contribute considerably to this. If the atmosphere were cleared, then a private non-committal exchange of views could perhaps first be entered upon, and this, if favorable, could be followed by more detailed talks and possibly negotiations. You had authorized these suggestions in principle, but attached decisive importance to secrecy; indiscretions could set everything back by five to ten years; any indiscreet reports would be most decidedly denied.

The Pope requested me to inform you that he would always be ready to pave the way for relations of friendship with Germany, a country very dear to him, as he has often emphasized already. We may rest assured of the discretion of the Curia. He would welcome it if, pending the final general settlement, further "harsh measures" could be avoided. (He was obviously thinking primarily of Austria (*Ostmark*).) The Pope, like you, apparently had in mind some kind of civil truce (*Burgfriede*) for the interim period. The Pope expressed concern about the international situation without going into details.[1]

It is interesting to note Bergen's insistence on the necessity for maintaining absolute secrecy about any rapprochement which might be reached. Ribbentrop appeared to be aware of the importance of having the support of the Sovereign Pontiff in the worsening international crisis; he was, perhaps, ready to give certain general promises concerning the religious policy of the Reich, but feared the reactions which such a backward step would provoke if it became known to his most bitter enemies inside the Party, who were at the same time the most bitter in their hostility to the Vatican—Göring and, even more, Goebbels and Rosenberg. At all events, Ribbentrop's was a skillful maneuver, because the Holy See was to lend its support to Reich diplomacy during the last weeks of the Polish crisis, judging, no doubt, that this was the only means of keeping the peace.

3. *The Holy See and the Polish Crisis*

At the beginning of the summer of 1939, relations between Berlin and Warsaw deteriorated sharply. Since March, Germany had been demanding the return of Danzig to the Reich. Obviously, this was to be only a first step which, as in the case of Czechoslovakia, would be followed by fresh claims,

[1] Letter from Bergen to Ribbentrop, June 9, 1939, *DGFP* (D, VI), pp. 690 f.

and these would lead, sooner or later, to the total subjugation of Poland. Colonel Joseph Beck answered Hitler's demands with a categorical refusal. On March 31, Great Britain guaranteed the frontiers of Poland. Any attack on that country might, therefore, mean a general European war.

On June 20, Ernst Woermann, Director of the Political Department of the Wilhelmstrasse, cabled to Ambassador Diego von Bergen:

¶ According to foreign press reports, Nuncio in Warsaw is to travel to Rome, or has already left, to convey to Pope Polish reply to his peace démarche. Nuncio is said to have had repeated discussions with Polish Foreign Minister in last few days which were allegedly concerned with Danzig question and possibility of friendly settlement of latter. Catholic circles in Poland reportedly taking favorable view of mediation by Vatican. Belief said to be held in Warsaw that if Vatican is satisfied with report from Warsaw Nuncio, it will now make démarche in Berlin.

Request report by telegram.

For your information. We learn from a very confidential source that Nuncio Warsaw carries instructions to recommend once again in discreet terms shrewdness and moderation in dealing with Germany. You may not utilize this information.[2]

That same day, Bergen replied that Msgr. Arnaldo Cortesi, the Nuncio at Warsaw, had just arrived in Rome and had immediately been received by the Cardinal Secretary of State. The tenor of the conversation was not yet known.[3]

[2] Telegram from Woermann to Bergen, June 20, 1939, StS: V, AA, Bonn (MS).
[3] Telegram from Bergen to Woermann, June 20, 1939, StS: V, AA, Bonn (MS).

Woermann's dispatch enables us to check the accuracy of the information reaching Berlin. As will be recalled, the last paragraph dealt with counsels of moderation given to the Poles by Msgr. Cortesi. Msgr. Giovanetti has revealed that the Holy See had received from Ciano an assurance that Germany did not intend to attack Poland. "On the strength of this fact," wrote Giovanetti, "the Vatican informed the Nuncio at Warsaw on June 6, 1939, that Germany had no intention at present of attacking Poland and urged him to repeat to the Polish Government the counsels of prudence which had been addressed to it by the Pope."[4]

By contrast, press reports to the effect that Warsaw desired mediation by the Pope were manifestly false. It seems, on the contrary, that the "slight" pressure exerted by the Holy See irritated the Poles.

On June 23, Hans Adolf von Moltke, the Ambassador of the Reich in Warsaw, reported more precise information on the relations between the Nuncio and Colonel Beck:

¶ Italian Ambassador here talked with Nuncio Cortesi a few days before his departure for Rome on June 17. Nuncio gave impression of being very dissatisfied and stated that in view of the intransigent Polish attitude he presently sees no possibility of compromise. It is true that this conversation took place before Nuncio's last discussion with Beck and before his audience with the President. However, from information to date, it cannot be assumed that these two conversations yielded any new factors on the political question. Count Szembek today made some critical remarks to an informant in reference to the action taken here a month ago by the Vatican, *which obviously conformed to the Ber-*

4 Giovanetti: op. cit., p. 88.

lin démarche,[5] and, when asked whether any new step was contemplated, answered only that the Vatican sometimes showed peculiar optimism . . .[6]

During the days that followed, Vatican policy became more firmly outlined, and when one recalls the talk between Pius XII and Bergen on June 9, one wonders if the information obtained on July 7 by Sir Percy Loraine, British Ambassador in Rome, from the Counselor of the Soviet Embassy there did not correspond to the calculations of the Holy See:

¶ . . . As regards the Vatican and Danzig, [wrote Percy Loraine] M. Helfand himself understands that concrete proposals have already been worked out in the Vatican and he fancies submitted to Berlin and Warsaw in the sense that Poland should admit not only that Danzig is a German City but also that it should revert to the Reich; and that in that case Herr Hitler should say that the formal taking over of Danzig by the Reich could be deferred for six or even twelve months in order to enable Germany and Poland meanwhile to reach an amicable agreement on the ways and means.

M. Helfand also said yesterday evening that the Vatican had already started negotiations with Germany for the regulation of position of Catholic Church in the Reich and he surmised the Vatican calculation to be that its successful mediation between Germany and Poland in the matter of Danzig would greatly assist its own negotiations with the German Government . . .[7]

---

5 Underlined by the German Ambassador.
6 Telegram from Moltke to Berlin, June 23, 1939, StS: V, AA, Bonn (MS).
7 Telegram from Percy Loraine to Halifax, July 7, 1939, *DBFP,* Third Series, VI, pp. 293 f.

The Cardinal Secretary of State, when informed of these statements by Osborne, British Ambassador to the Holy See, denied categorically that any plan of the kind existed and explained to Osborne that "all that the Vatican has done is to counsel moderation at Warsaw."[8] The truth appears to look somewhat different if one consults the memoirs of Colonel Beck:

¶ The initiatives of the Holy See were unfortunate, [wrote Beck]. At the instance of Msgr. Orsenigo, the Nuncio in Berlin, the Pope sent me, through the medium of Msgr. Cortesi, a confidential message in which he suggested that Poland should offer an arrangement favorable to the German minorities in Poland and made concrete proposals on this subject. I replied that these matters already had been discussed in the past between the Government of the Reich and ourselves, but always on a basis of reciprocity, and that we could accordingly consider such a démarche only if it had been made simultaneously, and in the identical form, in Berlin and if the Holy See were to inform us that the Government of the Reich was ready to make commitments of the same nature. The Nuncio never came back to this matter again.

In the closing days of August, the Pope approached us again, explaining that cession of Pomerania and Danzig could save the peace. I replied that publication of this démarche would offend the most sensitive feelings of the Catholic majority of citizens in our country. I added that our position had been clearly defined and that I left it to the discretion of the Holy See to decide whether or not it wished

[8] Telegram from Osborne to Halifax, July 8, 1939, ibid., p. 303.

to publish its démarche. The Nuncio subsequently thanked me for having handled the matter in this way.[9]

Beck's report is confirmed by a telegram which Osborne sent on August 30 to Halifax and also by the lines which Count Szembeck, Polish Undersecretary of State for Foreign Affairs, wrote in his diary on August 31. Together, these texts show the persistence with which the Vatican—less than a year after Munich—was experimenting along the same lines.

On August 30, Ambassador Osborne informed London that Cardinal Maglione had just acquainted him with the contents of a telegram sent to Warsaw:

¶ . . . Telegram states [wrote Osborne] that Vatican is informed that if Herr Hitler is assured of return of Danzig to the Reich he will be ready to negotiate on questions of Corridor and minorities and economic facilities for Poland at Danzig. The Nuncio is instructed to bring the above immediately to the personal attention of the President of Poland and to inform him that the Pope recommends this information to his most careful consideration . . .[1]

Next day, Count Szembek noted in his diary:

¶ Interview with Msgr. Cortesi:
By reason of the extreme gravity of the situation, which threatens to provoke immediate war, the Holy See has recommended him to state that the Vatican had received from highly authoritative sources information to the effect that if Poland would indicate a disposition to begin direct

[9] Joseph Beck: *Dernier Rapport, Politique Polonaise 1926–1939* (Neuchâtel: Éditions de la Baconnière; 1951), p. 213.
[1] Telegram from Osborne to Halifax, Aug. 30, 1939, *DBFP*, Third Series, VII, pp. 403 f.

conversations with the Reich and was not opposed to the return of Danzig to Germany, war could be avoided. The Holy See feels that eventual Polish-German conversations might relate to:

1. the return of Danzig to the Reich, assurances being given to Poland regarding commercial facilities which would be accorded to it in the Free City;
2. questions affecting the "Corridor";
3. matters concerning the German minorities in Poland.

With regard to the second point, I asked the Nuncio if this involved territorial claims by the Reich or was solely concerned with facilitating communications between East Prussia and the rest of Germany. Msgr. Cortesi replied that he did not know exactly and that the Polish Government could have the point clarified. The Nuncio then stressed that the Holy See was fully informed as to the Polish Government's view on the situation. Nevertheless, having regard to the danger of war, he felt he would be derelict in his duty if he failed to communicate this information. The Holy See wished to point out that, in doing so, it was animated solely by its special attachment to Poland and by its great fear of the danger of war.

The Holy See was, further, aware that if the Polish Government, having clearly outlined its attitude, were to show itself disposed to begin conversations with Berlin, and if the Reich rejected these, the whole world would turn away from the Reich, which would lose the support even of those who had backed it so far.

Interview with Beck:
I informed him of my conversation today with the Nuncio;

I detect here the hand of Mussolini. The Minister showed himself clearly opposed to this kind of mediation.[2]

It seems that the Pope also had thoughts of intervening directly without consulting the Poles. On August 29, the Führer had declared himself ready to negotiate if the Poles sent a plenipotentiary within twenty-four hours. This was an ultimatum which the Poles could not accept and which the British, though they conveyed the text to Warsaw, could not recommend the Poles to accept. On August 30, Weizsäcker noted in a memorandum addressed to Ribbentrop:

¶ The Italian Ambassador informed me this afternoon that he had heard from the British Ambassador that if a Polish negotiator failed to appear in Berlin, a new initiative was to be expected—an initiative by the Pope himself. This might contain positive suggestions analogous to the proposal made by the Führer in the spring of this year. Attolico told me this purely by way of information.[3]

A papal démarche in favor of a peaceful settlement took place on August 31; the convening of an international conference was suggested, but to no avail. On September 1, the Germans attacked Poland.

The first months of the pontificate of Pius XII coincided with the last months of peace in Europe. From the outset, the Sovereign Pontiff found himself confronted with a dramatic dilemma: while anxious to safeguard the interests of the Church in Germany and wishing to contribute to the maintenance of peace, he saw no way out except that of a policy of

[2] Jean Szembek: *Journal 1933–1939* (Paris: Plon; 1959), p. 499.
[3] Memorandum by Weizsäcker, Aug. 30, 1939, StS: V, AA, Bonn (MS).

extreme conciliation vis-à-vis the Reich. This led him to adopt toward Nazi Germany an attitude rather similar to that with which the name of Chamberlain was linked for several years. But in March 1939, the British Prime Minister changed his mind, while Pius XII, hoping that a dialogue with Hitler might still be possible, embarked on a course with unpredictable consequences.

Chapter II

THE VICTORIES
OF THE REICH

September 1939–June 1940

1. The Destruction of Poland

¶ We learn from a reliable source [wired Woermann to Bergen on September 6, 1939] that France and England are said to have insisted that Pope declare Germany the aggressor. Pope reported to have refused request, pointing to the traditional attitude of the Vatican which avoids direct intervention in international affairs. Main reason for refusal, however, said to be that Pope unwilling to impair situation of Catholics in Germany or prospects of his peace efforts and relations with Italy.[1]

The information Woermann had received was correct: Pius XII kept silence in the face of the German attack on Poland despite intervention by the Ambassadors of Great Britain and France at the Vatican. When, on September 1, Charles-Roux, the French Ambassador, tried to ascertain the attitude of the Holy See, Cardinal Maglione evaded the issue, saying: "The facts speak for themselves; let us first let them

[1] Telegram from Woermann to Bergen, Sept. 6, 1939, StS: V, AA, Bonn (MS).

[33]

speak."[2] The reasons for Pius XII's silence, as analyzed by Woermann, are probably accurate, but Bergen's response added a disturbing element. On September 7, the Reich Ambassador replied to Woermann:

¶ Pope's refusal to take sides against Germany would be entirely in harmony with assurances he has repeatedly conveyed to me through trusted agent in recent weeks.[3]

Bergen was saying, in other words, that during the crucial weeks of August the Pope, through an intermediary, had given him to understand that, if Germany attacked Poland, the Vatican would make no pronouncement against the Reich.

¶ In this grave hour, when our German people face a test of their resolve under fire and have come forward to fight for their natural and God-given rights, I address myself to you soldiers, you who are in the forefront of this battle and who have the honorable task of protecting and defending the security and life of the German nation with the sword . . . Each of you knows what is at stake for our people in these stormy days and each man sees before him, as he goes into action, the shining example of a true fighter, our Führer and Supreme Commander, the first and bravest soldier of the Greater German Reich, who is now with you at the fighting front.[4]

Such were the terms in which Msgr. Rarkowski, Chaplain General to the Wehrmacht, exhorted the soldiers of the

[2] François Charles-Roux: *Huit ans au Vatican, 1932–1940* (Paris: Flammarion; 1947), p. 339.
[3] Telegram from Bergen to Woermann, Sept. 7, 1939, StS: V, AA, Bonn (MS).
[4] Official Gazette of the Catholic Field Bishop to the Armed Forces, Vol. 3, 1939, p. 5; cf. Lewy: op. cit., p. 238.

Reich on the day Poland was attacked. A large majority of the German clergy at the various levels of the hierarchy shared the "ardent" sentiments of the Bishop of the armies. Any public statement by the Holy See of its attitude would henceforth create for it a further problem: the German Catholics, encouraged by their own Bishops and for the most part firm adherents of National Socialism, would probably turn aside from Rome if Pius XII openly condemned the Hitlerite aggression. Fear of an eventual schism among the German Catholics could not but drive the Sovereign Pontiff to new concessions, just as would his wish to avoid reprisals by the regime against loyal Catholics and, lastly, his hope of bringing about a restoration of peace.

Immediately after the liquidation of Poland, the desire to contribute to a return to peace led the Pope to support the offers made by Hitler and Mussolini. Obviously, a peace excluding a return to the *status quo ante* must inevitably have played into Germany's hands. Paris and London rejected the offers without hesitation. Just then the attitude of the Holy See—influenced no doubt by information from Poland concerning the fate reserved by the Germans for the civil population and the clergy of the country—stiffened for a moment.

On October 20, 1939, Pius XII, in his encyclical *Summi Pontificatus,* expressed his compassion for Poland, while refraining from an explicit condemnation of the German action. The Sovereign Pontiff declared, in particular:

¶ Venerable Brothers, it is, in many respects, *in your hour of darkness* (Luke 22, 53) that Our first Encyclical comes to you. The spirit of violence and of discord is bathing humanity in streams of blood and inexpressible suffering. Is there any need to assure you that Our paternal heart is with

[35]

all its sons and, more particularly, with the afflicted, the oppressed, and the persecuted?

The peoples who have been swept tragically into the vortex of war are perhaps only at the *beginning of sorrows* (Matt. 24, 8), but already, in thousands of families, desolation, misery, and death hold sway. The blood of countless human beings, noncombatants among them, has been shed and cries out to heaven, especially the blood of Poland, a nation very dear to us. Here is a people which has a right to the human and brotherly sympathy of the whole world, because of its devotion to the Church and by reason of the ardor it has poured into the defense of Christian civilization, so that its titles are carved indelibly in the tablets of history. And behold, Poland, confident in the powerful intercession of Mary, *"Auxilium Christianorum,"* awaits a return to the principles of true justice and peace which will bring the hour of resurrection.[5]

Before we evaluate the significance of this encyclical—and, incidentally, the significance of Nuncio Orsenigo's intervention on behalf of the Polish population, which we shall quote later—let us examine the Berlin reactions to the papal message. The Wilhelmstrasse documents provide résumés of them, but no more; a document in the archives of the Reich Chancellery, on the other hand, offers an interesting commentary. This occurs in a letter on the subject of the encyclical which was addressed by Reinhard Heydrich, Chief of the Security Police and the Security Service, on November 10, 1939, to Hans Lammers, Head of the Reich Chancellery (although the letter was signed by Heinrich Müller, Chief of the Gestapo). The major part of the letter was devoted to an

[5] Giovanetti: op. cit., p. 123.

accurate summary of the principal themes of the encyclical and quoted the most important passages. This was followed by a commentary:

¶ The encyclical is directed exclusively against Germany, both in ideology and in regard to the German-Polish dispute. How dangerous it is as regards our foreign relations as well as our domestic affairs is beyond discussion.

On the strength of various indications, it was expected that the encyclical would be read from the pulpits in the Reich on November 5, 1939. So far, however, only scattered reports have come in, according to which extracts of the encyclical have been read in the Aachen district and isolated readings have occurred in the Linz district and in Priesteritz-Wittenberg. The reading left no visible impression upon the listeners; on the contrary, the report of the State Police Office in Aachen says that the congregation followed the proceedings indifferently and without inner involvement.

That there was no further reading on November 5, 1939, may be due to the fact that up to that date the dioceses and individual parishes had not been informed in time and that further dissemination may be expected on Sundays to come. I have given instructions that, in pursuance of existing directives, readings of the encyclical in the churches are not to be hindered, but that all other forms of circulation, particularly by handbill, are to be stopped. The Reich Ministry for Popular Enlightenment and Propaganda has prohibited any discussion of the encyclical by the press, including the religious press.[6]

---

[6] Letter from Heydrich (signed by Müller) to Lammers, Nov. 10, 1939. Reich Chancellery Files, Federal Archives in Koblenz (MS).

The Sovereign Pontiff, in his first encyclical, raised his voice to condemn, implicitly, certain actions of the Reich, and to state, explicitly, his sympathy for the sufferings of one people *designated by name:* the Poles.

The Chief of the German Security Police considered the encyclical as being directed exclusively against Germany and as representing a manifest danger, in the context of both domestic and external affairs. What measures did he envisage? Reprisals against the priests who read out the encyclical? Reprisals against the German or Polish Catholics? Nothing of the kind. At the very most, dissemination of the encyclical in tract form and press comment would be prohibited.

This prudent reaction must be underlined, even though it cannot serve as a criterion of comparison for what might have happened subsequently. It seems, nevertheless—and the events that followed were to confirm this—that the Nazi leaders wished to avoid, for the duration of the war, an open and irremediable rupture with the Holy See, with all the consequences that this would involve.

Obviously, no German document gives any indication whether the encyclical *Summi Pontificatus,* or the intervention on the part of Msgr. Orsenigo which we are about to describe, had any favorable effect on the physical fate of the Poles who had been driven from their homes, but is it too much to suggest that many a Polish Catholic must have felt profound moral solace when he learned that the sufferings of his people were known and had led the Supreme Head of the Church to speak about them openly? But let us now turn to the intervention by the Nuncio in Berlin.

On November 29, Msgr. Orsenigo had a talk with Woermann, who noted down the most important points in the conversaton:

¶ The Nuncio today brought up the following points, emphasizing that he was speaking privately, [wrote Woermann on November 29]. Reports had come to him from various quarters, he said, relating to the treatment of Poles, particularly in the area of Posen [Poznan], but also in other parts of the . . . region. He knew, he said, that as Nuncio he was not entitled to bring up this matter, but he felt obliged as a human being to do so. . . . Things had recently occurred there which Germany, in its own interest, should not permit. He did not want to investigate here, he said, whether shootings of landowners which had taken place were justified or not; he was speaking only for the ordinary people. Women, children, and old people were being dragged from their beds by night and expelled, without having any other living quarters allotted to them. The Nuncio asked me if I could not advise him whom to approach in this matter.

I replied to the Nuncio that I could not recommend him to approach high-ranking German personalities because they would perhaps not listen to him as quietly as I had done and would at once object that, as Nuncio, he had no right to speak of these things. Moreover, I said, I firmly believed that he was the victim of false information. The Nuncio disputed the last point, stressing how cautious he was in evaluating reports. He asked me at least to have some discussion with the State Secretary as to whether something could not be done.[7]

The sufferings inflicted by the Germans on the people of Poland and their Church were known, then, in the Vatican. For this reason, the remarks which the Sovereign Pontiff was reported to have addressed to the Reich diplomats at the New

---

[7] Memorandum by Woermann, Nov. 29, 1939, StS: V, AA, Bonn (MS).

Year's reception are difficult to interpret. Bergen was absent and Menshausen, the Chargé d'Affaires, took his place:

¶ On occasion of customary New Year's receptions, I was received today in private audience by the Pope. He thanked me for the congratulations conveyed to him and asked that they be reciprocated most cordially to the Führer, the entire Reich Government and the dear German people. In this context, he recalled with warm words the long years of his stay in Germany, which at the time he had found it hard to leave. His great affection and love for Germany continued undiminished, he said, and perhaps he loved it all the more —if such a thing were at all possible—in these grave times.[8]

On January 1, Fritz Menshausen reported further on his audience with Pope Pius XII:

¶ In conversation, which the Pope extended beyond the limit prescribed by protocol, he made following statement—after expressing his unaltered affection for Germany:

The widespread notion that he was opposed to totalitarian states was inaccurate. Example of Italy demonstrated the opposite and proved that understanding and living on good terms entirely possible. Unfortunately, he said, he had waited in vain for a [. . .] that his own readiness, so often expressed, to reach an understanding, was reciprocated on the German side. When I remarked that papal pronouncements had been interpreted by the democratic Powers, without contradiction, as being directed against totalitarian states and had been exploited against us for propaganda purposes, the Pope replied that the exploitation for propaganda was surely occurring in reverse on the German side

[8] Telegram from Menshausen to Berlin, Dec. 31, 1939, StS: V, AA, Bonn (MS).

as well, in response to which I pointed out that our press had greater justice on its side. The Pope argued further that pronouncements were naturally only general in character and that, over and above this, he was always particularly concerned to phrase them in such a manner that they could not be misunderstood by Germany as being directed against that country . . .[9]

It is possible that the Pope feared he had committed himself too far in his encyclical *Summi Pontificatus* and wanted to use the opportunity provided by the New Year's audience to make an emphatic show of cordiality toward the German diplomats in order to revive the dialogue he had decided to maintain with the National-Socialist leaders. This is, of course, no more than a hypothesis which is obviously difficult to prove.

Moreover, at the end of 1939 and the beginning of 1940, when the Holy See could not fail to regard with disfavor the close relations prevailing between Berlin and Moscow, Pius XII seems to have adopted a complex attitude in regard to Germany which resulted in a number of parallel policies. This explains why, during the next few months, the Pope appears to have maintained contact with members of the German opposition to Hitler.[1]

2. Pius XII Meets Ribbentrop

ON MARCH 11, the day after his arrival in Rome, Ribbentrop, Reich Minister for Foreign Affairs, was received by the Pope. The following is an account of the conversation which was probably written by Ribbentrop himself:

[9] Telegram from Menshausen to Berlin, No. 159, Jan. 1, 1940, ibid.
[1] Cf., above all, Ulrich von Hassel: *Vom andern Deutschland* (Zurich: Atlantis Verlag; 1946), p. 140. See also Nobécourt: op. cit., pp. 193 ff.

¶ After the Reich Minister of Foreign Affairs had transmitted the Führer's greetings, the Pope began the conversation with a reference to his 17 years of activity in Germany. These years lived within the ambit of German culture had probably been, he said, the best years of his life, and the Reich Government could be certain that he had, and always would have, a warm place in his heart for Germany.

The Minister stressed that he would speak frankly and without diplomatic circumlocution, the Pope assenting vigorously. The Minister then took up the subject of the basic relationship between the National-Socialist State and the Catholic Church and expounded the German standpoint in the following terms:

The Führer, he said, was of the opinion that an agreement on fundamentals between National Socialism and the Catholic Church was entirely possible. However, there was no object in trying to regulate the relations between the two by tackling isolated questions of one kind or another or by making provisional arrangements. Rather, they must one day reach a comprehensive clarification—a secular clarification, as it were—of the relationship, which would then form a genuinely durable foundation for a harmonious interplay of the factors involved. But the time had not yet come for such a clarification. Germany was engaged in a struggle for existence which it would fight through to a victorious conclusion, no matter what happened, but which naturally was consuming all its energies and which did not permit the Führer to devote his attention to other problems. Moreover it must be borne in mind that an understanding between National Socialism and the Catholic Church depended on one cardinal prerequisite, namely, that the Catholic clergy

[42]

in Germany renounce political activity in any shape or form and confine themselves exclusively to the cure of souls, which alone was their concern. Today, the Catholic clergy in Germany do not as yet seem to have fully realized the necessity of so radical a distinction. Just as, in international politics, England had claimed for a long time a kind of tutelage over the Continent and the authority to interfere in all sorts of political problems of other countries, so the Catholic Church, in the course of its development, had become accustomed to interfering in politics. In Germany, he said, the Catholic Church had appropriated positions and powers of the most varied kind which, while the Church might regard them as rights properly acquired, could not be reconciled with the absolute necessity that the Church restrict itself to the cure of souls. The Catholic clergy must first allow themselves to be progressively convinced that the advent of National Socialism had brought into being an entirely new form of the state and the national life as a whole. Only when they had done so would it be possible to approach the task of thrashing out fundamentals and reaching an understanding with any hope of lasting success. We must not repeat an error such as the hasty conclusion of concordats (with the provincial administrations and with the Reich) which—if only because of the subsequent development of new constitutional forms in Germany—must already be considered out of date. In the Führer's opinion, therefore, the important thing for the time being was to maintain—and, if possible, extend—the existing truce. In this respect, very considerable advance concessions had been made on the German side. The Führer had quashed no fewer than 7,000 cases against Catholic priests. It should

[43]

also not be forgotten that the National-Socialist State was spending one billion Reichsmark[2] annually on the Catholic Church, an achievement of which no other state could boast.

The following, according to Ribbentrop, was the Sovereign Pontiff's reaction:

¶ The Pope showed understanding throughout of the statements made by the Reich Minister for Foreign Affairs and frankly conceded the facts mentioned. He tried of course, to turn the conversation to particular individual problems and complaints on the part of the Curia, but did not persist when the Minister emphasized again that a fundamental and all-embracing clarification of the whole field of relations between State and Church was necessary but would not be possible until later.

In conclusion, the Reich Minister for Foreign Affairs drew attention to the historic fact that never before in history had the stability of the Church been so little affected by a revolution as radical as that which National Socialism had produced in the entire life of the German people. On the contrary, it was, in the final analysis, only the assumption of power by National Socialism that had prevented the outbreak of Bolshevist chaos in Europe, by which religious life as such would have been destroyed. On the other hand, the Minister made it clear that the relationship between Germany and the Soviet Union had fundamentally changed. A firm and lasting basis for positive relations between the two countries had been created, and this had been made possible for National Socialism because the German people

2 About $400,000,000 at the exchange rate prevailing at the time. (Translator's note.)

were now immune to any form of Communist infection and because no further attempts were being made on the Soviet side to gain ground in Germany for the ideas of world revolution.

Ribbentrop then referred briefly to this talk with Secretary of State Maglione:

¶ In the ensuing talk between the Reich Minister for Foreign Affairs and Cardinal Maglione, the Secretary of State, the latter attempted to bring up a number of concrete questions for discussion, namely the problem of the confessional schools, permission for a representative of the Nuncio's office in Berlin to go to Warsaw, and maintenance payments from the Curia to Poland. The Minister did not enter into a factual discussion of the problem of confessional schools. He described the admission of diplomatic representatives to Warsaw in general terms as not yet possible and when the Cardinal Secretary of State began to speak, in this connection, of the necessity for a check on the use of Papal funds, the Minister rejected in very sharp language the implied suspicion cast on German officials, with the result that the Cardinal dropped this topic as well. On another matter raised by the Secretary of State, i.e., the question whether it was not possible to prevent the circulation of certain books hostile to the Church which had been published by the Ludendorff Verlag, the Minister, while not giving any positive assurance, held out the prospect that the facts would be investigated.[3]

In order to be able to make an objective analysis of the essential points of the interview between Pius XII and Ribben-

[3] Unsigned memorandum of Mar. 11, 1940, *DGFP* (D, VIII), pp. 896 f.

trop, one would like to read another version—namely, the version in the Vatican Archives. But it so happens that Msgr. Giovanetti—who, in the work often quoted here, draws copiously on those archives and includes lengthy passages on the talks between Ribbentrop and Cardinal Maglione regarding the concrete problems of the Church in Germany and Poland —passes over the interview between the Sovereign Pontiff and the Reich Minister for Foreign Affairs in a few words, though these words are significant:

¶ A few hours earlier [before the interview with Maglione], during the interview which he had been granted, he (Ribbentrop) had been able to observe with deep satisfaction that the Pope's heart was still in Germany and that he displayed great goodwill in the matter of reaching an understanding.[4]

This curious reticence on the part of Msgr. Giovanetti may be explained by the fact that the Vatican record of the talk confirms, perhaps, the main points reported by Ribbentrop, namely:

The interview took place in a cordial atmosphere, and the Pope, in opening the conversation, showed once more his lively sympathy for Germany;

The Pope did not dwell on the concrete complaints of the Holy See against the Reich and probably accepted Ribbentrop's basic idea to the effect that a settlement of the relations between the Holy See and the Reich could be effected only on a global basis after the war was over.

In conclusion, one more hypothesis suggests itself: Certain political plans may possibly have been discussed which Ribbentrop, having regard to the relations then existing

[4] Giovanetti: op. cit., p. 177.

between the Reich and Russia, could not record in his memorandum, but which nothing prevented the Sovereign Pontiff from entrusting to the Vatican Archives. These plans—which Msgr. Giovanetti mentions only to deny them—were exposed by Camille Cianfarra, the *New York Times* correspondent in Rome, who probably gained knowledge of them through one of his informants in the Vatican. According to him, Ribbentrop and the Pope had discussed the possibility of a return to peace based on recognition of a *de facto* German hegemony in Central and Eastern Europe, and the possibility of a "liberation of Russia."[5]

Although this hypothesis is difficult to check, it cannot be entirely excluded, particularly when one remembers the terms of the address delivered by Pius XII on October 18, 1939, when he received the new Lithuanian Minister to the Holy See:

¶ Being conscious of the duties inherent in Our office of Supreme Pastor and even though not solicited to refrain from so doing, [declared the Pope] We shall not allow Our actions—directed, as they always are, at the salvation of souls—to become involved in purely temporal controversies and territorial rivalries among states. But the very duty of Our office does not permit us to close Our eyes when new and immeasurable dangers threaten that salvation itself; when the face of Europe, Christian in all its fundamental traits, is darkened by a sinister shadow, closer and more menacing every day—the shadow of the thought and works of the enemies of God. In such circumstances, more than at any other period of history, the preservation, the cultivation and, if need be, the defense of the Christian heritage

5 Camille M. Cianfarra: *The War and the Vatican* (New York: Dutton; 1944), pp. 209 f.

acquire capital importance for the future destiny of Europe and the prosperity of all its peoples, great or small.

In quoting these remarks, Msgr. Giovanetti wrote that the Pope was alluding "to the terrible menace of atheistic Communism and deemed it his pastoral duty to draw attention to its peril."[6]

3. The Invasion of Belgium, Holland, and Luxembourg

ON MAY 10, Belgium, Holland, and Luxembourg were invaded, and the Pope abandoned his reserve. That same day, he addressed a message to the sovereigns of the three countries that had been attacked.

To King Leopold, the Sovereign Pontiff wrote:

¶ At this moment when the Belgian people, against their will and contrary to their right, see their territory exposed for the second time to the cruelties of war, We are profoundly moved, and We send to Your Majesty and all your well-beloved nation the assurance of Our paternal affection; and as We pray to Almighty God that this sore trial may end with the restoration of Belgium's full liberty and independence, We bestow upon Your Majesty and his people, with all Our heart, Our apostolic blessing.

To Queen Wilhelmina:

¶ Having learned with intense emotion that Your Majesty's efforts for peace have not succeeded in preserving a noble people from becoming involved in a theater of war, We beseech God, the Supreme Arbiter of the destinies of na-

6 Giovanetti: op. cit., pp. 142 f.

tions, to hasten by His almighty aid the restoration of peace and liberty.[7]

On May 11, Bergen wired to Berlin:

¶ From a source well informed about Pope's intentions, I hear that Pope's telegrams to King of the Belgians, Queen of the Netherlands and Grand Duchess of Luxembourg, published this evening in *L'Osservatore Romano,* are not to be construed as political intervention, let alone unilateral condemnation of German action. Pronouncements contained no word of protest. Pope had merely intended to express to the heads of state and peoples concerned his sorrow at the fact that they were being drawn into the conflict against their will and were being directly affected by the hardships of war.

Message to the King of the Belgians is not a reply to his appeal to Pius XII making one-sided charges against Germany, but crossed it.[8]

Next day, Ambassador Dino Alfieri was instructed to protest to the Pope in the name of the Duce. Hans Georg von Mackensen, the Ambassador of the Reich at the Quirinal, reported what the Italian diplomat had told him of his talk with Pius XII:

¶ Alfieri told me very confidentially during farewell visit today that in the course of his farewell audience with the Pope he told the latter in serious terms, on the Duce's instructions, that Pope's telegrams to Belgium and Holland had had a very painful effect on the Duce. Pope countered that

---

[7] Paul Duclos: *Le Vatican et la Seconde Guerre Mondiale* (Paris: Pedone; 1955), p. 59.
[8] Telegram from Bergen to Berlin, May 11, 1940, StS: V, AA, Bonn (MS).

in the telegrams, which were the result of hours of reflection, he had spoken only as the Supreme Pontiff standing aloof from all mundane happenings and had scrupulously avoided any word of political import, such as "invasion," that might imply a viewpoint. Alfieri said he had replied that such a separation between the priesthood and politics was impossible, because the mere fact that the telegrams were sent was a political act. Moreover, he said, the Pope must not forget that there were 30 million Catholics living in the Reich. The interview, Alfieri thought, had been "very tough."[9]

Some days later, Alfieri arrived in Berlin to become the new Italian Ambassador. During his first visit to Woermann, he reported details of his interview with the Pope; his account tallied in the main with the details he had already supplied to Mackensen, but he added one important point:

¶ The Pope, he said, had been astonished that there were objections to the attitude of *L'Osservatore Romano* and had promised to give instructions again that this journal was not to take sides clearly in favor of Britain and France . . .

Then the Ambassador added:

¶ . . . that both Germany and Italy had an interest in being on good terms with the Vatican, at least for the duration of the War. What would come afterwards remained to be seen.[1]

Finally, Alfieri related his conversation with the Pope in his memoirs, adding a detail often quoted since:

¶ The duties inherent in my office made it necessary to express, in accordance with instructions received from Ciano,

9 Telegram from Mackensen to Berlin, May 13, 1940; ibid. (MS).
1 Memorandum by Woermann, May 19, 1940, *DGFP* (D, IX), p. 378.

the Duce's regret at the prominence which the Catholic newspapers, and in particular *L'Osservatore Romano,* had given
to the three telegrams sent by the Holy Father to the King
of the Belgians, the Queen of Holland, and the Grand Duchess of Luxembourg following "the unjust invasion of their
territories by Nazi troops."

The Holy Father replied that he found the Duce's irritation incomprehensible . . . "Whatever happens in the future,"
concluded the Holy Father calmly but firmly, "even if they
come and take me off to a concentration camp, I have absolutely nothing with which to reproach myself. Every man
will be answerable to God for his own actions."[2]

The first thought that impresses itself on the mind as one
reads these texts is the same as that which could have been
prompted by the encyclical *Summi Pontificatus.* The Pope,
who had been moved to express his pain at the sufferings of
Poland, this time voiced his emotion to the Belgians, the Dutch,
and the Luxembourgers. Why would he keep silent when
there were Jews involved? Perhaps, at this stage, we may suggest the first ingredient of an answer which will doubtless
contain other, more important elements. This part of the answer is supplied to us by an article in *L'Osservatore Romano,*
published a few weeks before the German attack in Flanders
and immediately after the aggression of the Reich against
Denmark and Norway, two small, neutral states. The Pope
refrained from any reaction. Yet, was not the situation similar to that which arose out of the attack on Belgium, Holland,
and Luxembourg? *L'Osservatore Romano* enables us to grasp
the difference when, in an article attempting to justify the

---

[2] Dino Alfieri: *Dictators Face to Face* (New York: New York Uni-
versity Press; 1955), pp. 16 f.

silence of the Sovereign Pontiff in the face of the events in Scandinavia, the organ of the Vatican writes:

¶ There are only 2,000 Catholics in Norway; that being so, the Holy See, though severely condemning the moral aspect of the matter, must take a practical view and bear in mind the 30 million German Catholics.[3]

Now, in Belgium the population is predominantly Catholic; there are also numerous Catholics in Holland and Luxembourg; the same is true of Poland. Though one hesitates to draw a conclusion, one cannot entirely dismiss the question: Did not the Sovereign Pontiff openly condemn violence and aggression only when the victims were Catholics? This hypothesis is not tendentious. It simply implies that the Pope conceived his duty within very narrow limits.

Moreover, the Sovereign Pontiff's caution grew more marked, keeping pace with the rhythm of the German victories. On May 18, Bergen supplied new data on the interpretation which the Vatican henceforth would place on the three telegrams:

¶ . . . was intimated at the office of the Secretary of State that Pope, foreseeing King Leopold's telegram, wanted to anticipate it and avoid answering. In this connection, it was emphasized that telegrams were not intended as any kind of barb against Germany.[4]

The Vatican radio emphasized on May 21, in an English-language broadcast,[5] that in his messages and words the Pope

[3] Duclos: op. cit., pp. 58 f.
[4] Telegram from Bergen to Berlin, May 18, 1940, StS: V, AA, Bonn (MS).
[5] It has not been possible to find any reference to that broadcast cited by Bergen.

had always deliberately refrained from showing any particular sympathy for, or adopting an attitude toward, one of the belligerents.⁶ On May 16, *L'Osservatore Romano* had terminated its political commentaries.⁷

4. The Defeat of France

AT THE END of May 1940, the battle of France was not yet irretrievably lost by the Allies. On the 27th, Bergen informed the Wilhelmstrasse that he had just learned "from a very confidential source" that:

¶ The view was being expressed today in the Office of the Secretary of State that it would be best if France were to sign a separate peace and that Britain should be left to fight on alone.⁸

On the 29th, Bergen sent an even more tersely worded telegram:

¶ According to my very confidential information, the view in the Office of the Papal Secretary of State is that Belgium would have been well advised to capitulate and that France should do the same.⁹

On June 8, the Ambassador of the Reich sent a confirmatory message:

¶ Opinion in the Vatican has been, and still is, that France should follow the example of Belgium.¹

⁶ Telegram from Bergen to Berlin, May 22, 1940, ibid. (MS).
⁷ Duclos: op. cit., p. 61.
⁸ Telegram from Bergen to Berlin, May 27, 1940, *DGFP* (D, IX), p. 144.
⁹ Telegram from Bergen to Berlin, May 29, 1940, StS: V, AA, Bonn (MS).
¹ Telegram from Bergen to Berlin, June 8, 1940, ibid. (MS).

On June 10, a few hours before Italy entered the war, Nuncio Orsenigo called on Woermann. The latter described the conversation thus:

¶ The Nuncio called on me today in connection with current matters. In the conversation, he gave very cordial expression to his pleasure at the German victories. It seemed as if he could not wait for Italy to enter the War and he remarked jokingly that he hoped the Germans would march into Paris by way of Versailles.[2]

A reading of these texts contributes to a better understanding of the atmosphere prevailing in the Vatican at the beginning of June 1940, and in this context the letter sent by Eugène Cardinal Tisserant to Emmanuel Cardinal Suhard on June 11 acquires new contours:

¶ Most Eminent and Reverend Sir:
I received yesterday the letter which Your Eminence addressed to me on the 4th. My sincere thanks for the kindness which Your Eminence is good enough to show me; if we survive this trial, I shall, when passing through Paris, gladly take advantage of the hospitality you offer me. But what will happen between now and then? I had foreseen since August 28 what happened yesterday and I told General Georges as much when I met him at the end of December. How shall we be able to resist this new danger? May God help us and help you.

The Cardinal was evidently referring to Italy's entry into the war on the previous day which had been the object of Msgr. Orsenigo's prayers. Cardinal Tisserant continued:

¶ In any event, let the French be under no illusions: what

2 Memorandum by Woermann, June 10, 1940, ibid. (MS).

their enemies want is their destruction. These past few days, the Italian press has been full of statements by His Excellency Signor Mussolini saying: We are prolific and we want land! And that means uninhabited land. Germany and Italy therefore will direct all their efforts at destroying the inhabitants of occupied regions, as they have done in Poland. Instead of dying on the battlefield, Frenchmen will be obliged to die by inches—men separated from their wives, and children spared, perhaps, to serve their conquerors as slaves, for, to our enemies, such is the law of war. Our governments will not understand the true nature of the conflict and persist in imagining that this is a war like the wars of times gone by. But Fascist ideology and Hitlerism have transformed the consciences of the young, and those under thirty-five are willing to commit any crime for any purpose ordered by their leader.

In this remarkable passage, Cardinal Tisserant defines, if not the nature of Italian Fascism, surely the very essence of German National Socialism. His definition certainly fell short of reality because the human imagination has limits: "children spared" . . . "a slow death" . . . But the lines that follow are the most shattering because they have a direct bearing on the attitude of the Pope:

¶ Since the beginning of November, I have persistently requested the Holy See to issue an encyclical on the duty of the individual to obey the dictates of conscience, because this is the vital point of Christianity; whereas Islam—which served as a model for Hitler, thanks to Hess, the son of a Moslem mother—substitutes for the individual conscience the duty to obey blindly the orders of the prophet or of his successors.

I fear that history may have reason to reproach the Holy See with having pursued a policy of convenience to itself and very little else. This is sad in the extreme, particularly when one has lived under Pius XI. And everyone is counting on the fact that, Rome having once been declared an open city, no one in the Curia would have to suffer; this is ignominious. It is all the more ignominious because the Secretariat of State and the Nuncio have persuaded large numbers of nuns and monks [the monks in question are French] not to leave, so as to provide Italy with hostages. And yet Rome is an entrenched camp, surrounded by a chain of forts, which have always been manned by troops, and it contains two large arms plants, a cartridge factory and an artillery repair shop! But those people [the Italians], like the Germans, will hide their staff headquarters under the Geneva Cross, which the British and the French ought to say they can no longer recognize since it does not protect our hospitals.[3]

5. *The Path of Concessions*

FOR CARDINAL TISSERANT, the logic of Pius XII's concessions was difficult to admit, because he glimpsed what would become of a Europe dominated by German National Socialism. Was the Pope himself unaware of this? Doubtless not entirely, because ever since the autumn of 1939 disturbing reports had been reaching him from Poland. In the spring

[3] Letter from Cardinal Tisserant to Cardinal Suhard, June 11, 1940, found by the Germans when looting the Archbishop's Palace in Paris, and forwarded by Heydrich to Lammers on Sept. 25, 1940. It was discovered in the archives of the Reich Chancellery (now stored in the *Bundesarchiv* at Koblenz) by Professor E. Jaeckel and first published in his article "Zur Politik des Heiligen Stuhls im Zweiten Weltkrieg," *Geschichte in Wissenschaft und Unterricht,* January 1964.

of 1940 the Holy See was even better informed: on March 15, 1940, State Secretary Weizsäcker recorded a talk that he had just had with Nuncio Orsenigo:

¶ The Nuncio today again brought up the subject of the priests in Sachsenhausen.

I told the Nuncio from the outset that I should not like to raise any hopes in him that his wish to visit the priests in Sachsenhausen would be fulfilled.

The Nuncio resigned himself to this, but made the following points:

There was to his knowledge a sick bay in Sachsenhausen in which Catholic priests, among others, were housed. He asked that:

1. a priest, to be selected by the Government, be granted permission to give comfort and administer the last sacraments to the invalids there;
2. that priests who die not be cremated because cremation is completely contrary to the principles of the Church;
3. that the priests be allowed to receive a breviary, and that they be permitted to celebrate mass among themselves in a cell placed at their disposal, without outside help and without the introduction of any strange priests.[4]

At the beginning of June, Pius XII had a talk with Signor Soro, former Secretary in the Italian Embassy in Warsaw:

¶ I hear that Secretary Soro of the former Italian Embassy in Warsaw, who was there until about the end of April with the task of winding up business, was received in private

[4] Memorandum by Weizsäcker of March 15, 1940, StS: V, AA, Bonn (MS).

audience by the Pope a short time ago. During their talk, Pope stated he knew very well that the innumerable inflammatory rumors about conditions in the General Government were partially exaggerated. He asked Soro to inform him, if he could do so without being indiscreet, whether constantly recurring rumors of sterilization of Polish women and girls were based on fact; whether these women and girls were being transported away to German brothels; and whether there were increasing cases of their being raped by German occupation troops. Soro denied this vigorously, pointing out that from his uninterrupted stay in Warsaw conditions there were very well known to him; that he himself had often followed up individual cases and had always discovered the rumors to be unfounded. . . .[5]

Was the Sovereign Pontiff duped by the denials of the Italian diplomat? The questions he asked indicate that he was probably informed.

Up to the beginning of the summer of 1940, the attitude of Pius XII seems to have been dictated by the considerations we have already stressed and, from the outbreak of the war, essentially by a desire to avoid any statement that would lead the German Catholics to turn away from Rome.

At the end of June 1940, a new element—later to become decisive—appeared to influence the Pope's attitude: the Soviet menace.

[5] Telegram from Bergen to Berlin, June 6, 1940, StS: V, AA, Bonn (MS).

Chapter III

THE BEGINNING OF
THE NEW ORDER IN EUROPE

June 1940–June 1941

---

1. Mediation by Pius XII and the Soviet Menace

O N JUNE 28, 1940, Bergen sent Ribbentrop the following top secret personal telegram:

¶ Cardinal Secretary of State summoned me today and handed me message from the Pope, given in translation below, with the request that it be forwarded soonest to the Führer and Reich Chancellor.

"Deeply concerned at the prospect of the numberless victims and the irretrievable devastation to which the renewal of hostilities, now imminent, will lead; acting on his own initiative and with the sole purpose of putting forth his utmost effort to save humanity and civilization; convinced that a just and honorable peace is the wish of the nations and that the War may easily bring further struggles and crises in its train; the Holy Father would like to address himself to the Governments of Germany, Britain, and Italy with the request that they seek the paths of mutual understanding in order to bring about a cessation of the conflict. Before embarking on this step, however, His Holiness wishes Your Excellency to inquire in confidence of your Government what reception such a request from the Pope might receive at its hands."

Same démarche was made to Italian Ambassador. Analogous communication will go to British Government through Apostolic Delegate in London as British Minister to the Holy See here has no means of communication with his Government.

Cardinal Secretary of State stressed orally once more that intention of Pope to mediate based absolutely on own initiative . . .

I should be grateful for instructions for purpose of answering inquiry.[1]

Now for several days, Hitler, on his part, had been taking a multiplicity of steps to induce England to accept a cessation of hostilities.

On June 14, he granted to Karl von Wiegand, the American journalist, an interview in which he declared, notably, that he had no desire to destroy Great Britain nor even to harm its empire. Simultaneously, the Germans approached a variety of mediators, such as Prince von Hohenlohe, Burckhardt, the former League of Nations High Commissioner in Danzig, some Swiss diplomats, etc.

The Pope's démarche was certainly motivated by a desire to restore peace. The fact remains, nonetheless, that if Great Britain had agreed to sign a peace in June 1940, German

---

[1] Telegram from Bergen to Ribbentrop, June 28, 1940, *DGFP* (D, X), p. 49.

hegemony over the whole of continental Europe would have been assured. It is possible that Pius XII glimpsed this danger, but decided nevertheless to support the efforts of the Germans on account of what seemed to him an even graver danger: an expansion of the Soviet Union into Europe.

At the very moment when France capitulated, the Soviet Union annexed the Baltic countries and, a few days later, forced Romania to cede Bessarabia and Northern Bucovina to Russia. The Pope realized, without a doubt, that if the Reich continued its efforts to bring down Great Britain in a struggle which might be long and difficult, the Russians could profit from this by extending even further their domination of Eastern Europe. It is, perhaps, not altogether outside the realm of possibility that Pius XII believed that a peace between Berlin and London would eventually enable the Reich to turn on the Soviet Union and rid that country of atheistic Communism. (It should be made clear that we have no document written in 1940 indicating such an intention and that this is a mere hypothesis on my part.)

On July 3, Nuncio Orsenigo made soundings at the Wilhelmstrasse as to whether anything was known there of Britain's attitude regarding the Pope's démarche. Weizsäcker replied that he knew nothing more than was being said in official British speeches, which seemed uncompromising. As for Germany's attitude, the State Secretary avoided a direct answer: the Reich, he explained, was continuing its preparations for an attack on England.[2]

On July 19, Hitler made official peace proposals to Great Britain in a major speech in the Reichstag. The British reply

[2] Memorandum from Weizsäcker, July 3, 1940, StS: V, AA, Bonn (MS).

was not slow in coming: "We shall continue the struggle," proclaimed Lord Halifax on July 21, "until liberty is assured."

On July 26, Weizsäcker informed the Nuncio of the Reich's reply to Pius XII's message:

¶ We had believed for some time, I said, that we were sufficiently well informed as to the response from London to the Curia's soundings on the question of peace to have to regard the British attitude as negative.

Germany's answer to the soundings of the Curia had, in effect, been expressed in the Führer's speech on the 19th of this month. The answer made by Lord Halifax in his radio address of the 21st fully confirmed our view regarding the obduracy of the British Government. Obviously, I said, England simply wanted war, and war it would get with all its horrors.

The Nuncio, for his part, also found Britain's stubbornness incomprehensible. By contrast, he fully acknowledged the unequivocal nature of the Führer's statements. Now, he supposed, there was nothing more to be said. It always took two to make a marriage.[3]

The war went on.

2. *An Unfathomable Personality*

IT WILL BE REMEMBERED that on the occasion of the the New Year's audience at the end of December 1939, Pius XII, in spite of disturbing information coming in from Poland, had manifested very marked cordiality toward the German diplomats. We have suggested that the Sovereign Pontiff wished to soften the possible effect of the encyclical *Summi*

[3] Memorandum by Weizsäcker of July of 26, 1940, ibid. (MS).

Pontificatus, in order to maintain the dialogue with the Reich. The documents we shall now present are less easy to explain.

In the course of the summer and fall of 1940, details concerning arrests of Polish priests streamed into the Vatican. On September 20, 1940, Weizsäcker described a conversation with the Apostolic Nuncio on this subject:

¶ The Nuncio raised the following matter with me today: According to information reaching him, arrests of priests in several waves, and amounting so far to about 200 persons, had occurred a short time ago at many places in what used to be Poland (he named Gnesen, Posen and Kutno). Many parishes had been left untended. Though he had been unable to check these reports, he feared that they were accurate. No reason for the arrests had been brought to his notice. He had hoped the cases concerned would be temporary measures, but it appeared that the arrested men had been taken to Dachau or Oranienburg. Should the reports be confirmed, which he asked me to investigate, he would be grateful if reasons could be given. He would assume that the measures involved were those of subordinate officials and not the result of instructions from any central authority.[4]

On November 26, a report from the Security Police confirmed the details submitted to Weizsäcker by the Nuncio:

¶ In reply to the foregoing question, [wrote a Gestapo functionary to Minister Luther] I would inform you that a number of Polish Catholic priests were taken into custody some time ago in the incorporated Eastern Territories. The measures concerned, however, were taken not as a general procedure but as various single actions whose execution was

[4] Minute by Weizsäcker, Sept. 20, 1940, StS: V, Bonn (MS).

considered an urgent necessity by the Secret Police for security reasons. Only those priests were arrested who either had taken part in activity inimical to the State or who, by the outward display of their pro-Polish attitude, were endeavoring to disrupt constructive German efforts.

The measures taken were, therefore, urgently necessary for the maintenance of public security and order.

I would add that an adequate number of Catholic priests are still carrying out their duties in the areas in question, so that pastoral care of both the German Catholic and Polish Catholic elements of the population is assured in every way.[5]

On December 11, Msgr. Orsenigo again approached Weizsäcker about the arrested priests:

¶ The Nuncio asked me today [wrote the State Secretary] whether the transfer of the Catholic priests in concentration camps to Dachau was already in progress. I was unable to give him any information about this.

The Nuncio remarked casually that he believed a rather large room resembling a chapel was being built for these priests in Dachau. He mentioned this happily.[6]

These were the circumstances in which the Pope received the German Ambassador for a New Year's audience on January 16:

¶ In the New Year's audience granted to me today, I repeated the good wishes of the Führer and the Reich Government in person.

Pius XII asked me to transmit his sincere thanks; he

[5] Memorandum by Department IV A 4 a of the Security Police to Luther of Nov. 26, 1940, StS: V, AA, Bonn (MS).
[6] Memorandum by Weizsäcker, Dec. 11, 1940, ibid. (MS).

reciprocated the good wishes, he said, for the Führer, the Government and all the German people. He made particular mention of the Reich Minister for Foreign Affairs whose visit last year he remembered with pleasure. In the course of the conversation, which otherwise was of a private nature, I observed that in my view a general settlement of pending questions could not take place until after the conclusion of the War. The Pope nodded agreement and indicated that the Reich Minister of Foreign Affairs had expressed himself in this sense.

Subsequently, I presented members of the Embassy to the Pope; he greeted them all in a most friendly manner and then made a short address to us in German, using warm words to express good wishes, and joyfully recalled his long sojourn in Germany, with which, he said, he was linked by the most beautiful memories.[7]

On March 24, Bergen wrote to the Wilhelmstrasse:

¶ Influential Italian friends are constantly and most urgently calling my attention to rumors making the rounds here, allegedly utilized by the London radio, according to which inmates of insane asylums and homes for the aged in Germany have been eliminated by being put to sleep or by restriction of food rations, and have been made the subjects of experimentation with poison gas. Their families have received either their ashes or else sentimental letters to the effect that every care and medical art had unfortunately not been able to save the patient. The number of victims so far amounts to many thousands.

As early as November of last year I heard from a confidential informant that no report out of Germany and the

[7] Telegram from Bergen, Jan. 16, 1941, StS: V, AA, Bonn (MS).

occupied areas had so shaken and grievously moved the Pope as this; he had had masses read for those persons whose names had been given to him. I have rejected the rumors at once as figments of the imagination of enemy propaganda.

At the beginning of December 1940 the Holy Office published the decision reported in dispatch A. 848 of December 6, 1940, according to which it is not permitted "by order of the government to kill persons who—are judged to be a burden to the congregation and a hindrance to its strength and power."[8] It was obviously brought about by the alleged procedures in Germany.

While registering a protest to a Vatican radio program I noted a remark dropped at the responsible office that there were much more grave reports which, out of consideration for Germany, had not been published either in the Vatican press or on the Vatican radio.

I should like to suggest that these enemy propaganda rumors, that are exceedingly damaging to us in public opinion here, be emphatically countered at some opportunity.[9]

On March 21, the Reich Minister in Lisbon reported:

¶ Today's *A Voz* reported under Vatican dateline that seven hundred Catholic priests had been shot in the concentration camps at Oranienburg, Dachau, Buchenwald and Os-

[8] The decision of the Holy Office to which Bergen alludes is dated December 2 (not 6) and runs as follows: "It is forbidden to kill, at the order of the state authority, people who have committed no crime incurring the death penalty but who, purely by reason of a psychological or physical sickness, can no longer be of use to the nation and who may even be regarded as a burden and an obstacle to the vigorous development of the community." *Acta Apostolicae Sedis*, 1940, p. 553. It should be noted, however, that this text was neither published in *L'Osservatore Romano* nor broadcast by the Vatican Radio. The *Acta* are written in Latin.

[9] Telegram from Bergen to Berlin, March 24, 1941, *DGFP* (D, XII), pp. 347 f.

wiecim [Auschwitz] and that there are still another three thousand Catholic priests in concentration camps.[1]

The information was correct. On March 4, at the very moment when information was coming into the Vatican concerning the killing of thousands of mental patients and hundreds of Polish priests, the German Ambassador in Rome sent the following personal report to Ribbentrop:

¶ Dr. Erich von Prittwitz-Gaffron, the artistic adviser of General Manager Tietjen, has just visited me and submitted the following information on the latter's behalf:

"Yesterday, March 3, a representative of the Pope appeared in General Manager Tietjen's office and, acting on the former's direct instructions, informed him that the Pope would be extremely pleased if, at the end of the guest performance of the Berlin State Opera in Rome, a concert by the State Orchestra could be arranged in the Vatican to present a concert version of the last scene of the music drama *Parsifal*. The Pope indicated through his plenipotentiary that he knew the State Opera's high level of artistry from the time when he was acting as Nuncio in Berlin and had often had the opportunity to admire the great Wagner productions staged under the direction of General Manager Tietjen . . ."[2]

On March 6, Ribbentrop gave his consent.

The *Civiltà Cattolica*, in its issue of March 1965, published the following additional details on this subject. On March 7, 1941, Monsignor Montini, the Undersecretary of State, sent a memorandum to the Sovereign Pontiff reporting

1 Telegram from Huene to Berlin, March 21, 1941, StS: V, AA, Bonn (MS).
2 Telegram from Mackensen to Ribbentrop, March 4, 1941, StS: V, AA, Bonn (MS).

on the manner in which the German Embassy had presented the matter to the Vatican:

¶ M. Erich von Prittwitz und Gaffron, accompanied by M. Tannstein, an attaché at the Embassy of Germany to the Holy See, came this evening to the office of the Secretary of State and said that a person unknown to him had told M. Heinz Tietjen, the General Manager of the Prussian State Theater, that the Holy Father would like to hear the last scene of *Parsifal*. The Reich Government at once showed interest in the matter, made it known that it would be most willing to meet the wish of his Holiness and arranged immediately for the artists present in Rome to be placed at M. Tietjen's disposal for this purpose. The musical scores were requested forthwith from Berlin and they will arrive in Rome tomorrow morning by air. M. Tietjen, who is supposed to be known to the Holy Father, considers himself greatly honored to have the opportunity, with his artists, to perform this piece of German music before His Holiness. M. von Prittwitz, too, expresses his satisfaction in enthusiastic terms; he is the brother of the (present?) Ambassador of the Reich to the United States and he knew the Holy Father in Berlin where he was working in connection with the Carnegie Foundation.

The concert cannot take place until Tuesday, the 11th of this month, because the artists are booked for other concerts and performances on all the other days, and they have to leave on Wednesday. Two soloists, some 100 musicians and 100 members of the chorus are involved. A decision as to the choice of the salon in which the concert is to take place is urgent in order that all the necessary arrangements may be made to ensure the concert's complete success. M. von Tannstein would like to be informed this evening or by about eleven a.m. tomorrow which salon has been chosen so that he may be able to go there with the conductor of the orchestra.

Msgr. Montini had written this note to give Pius XII an account of the interview. Here, now, is the memorandum in which he recorded what the Pope then said to him and which the Pope subsequently corrected in his own hand (Pius XII's corrections are in thin writing):

¶ His Holiness wishes to make it clear that the facts of the matter are very different. He had received through Father Grisar a letter from the parish priest of one of the artists, with a recommendation from the archbishopric. In this letter, an audience was requested for some Catholic performers who would be joined by a few Protestants. At this audience, they proposed in addition to perform some small item of music, presented on a limited basis, and they mentioned the last scene of *Parsifal* or of a "Stabat Mater." The Holy Father sent a reply to the effect that he would be glad to grant the audience; as for the musical performance, he would prefer a passage from the St. Matthew Passion by Bach, which would be more in keeping with the prevailing Lenten season. It is, therefore, inaccurate to say that the Holy Father took the initiative in the matter and that he suggested the Wagner segment indicated above; this was not at all because he does not have a high opinion of that composer but because the other piece proposed, by Bach, seemed more appropriate. In any event, the musical performance was to be an addition to the audience requested by the artists themselves.

His Holiness requests that all this shall be clarified, and he adds, rectifying something which has been loudly proclaimed by M. von Prittwitz, that the Holy Father was never present at any theatrical performance in Berlin, and that he does not remember ever having heard the Wagner passage represented as being a favorite of the Holy Father's. He recalls having attended two concerts in an official capacity at a time when the anniversary of the Weimar Constitution was being celebrated, on which occasion performances were given of, among other things, the Eroica Symphony and the Ninth Symphony of Beethoven; he does not recall that Wagner's *Parsifal* was played. He heard the St. Matthew Passion by Bach in Munich.

His Holiness wonders whether the audience, including a musical performance of some kind, can now be refused; it is, however, essential that it take place without invitations being issued, and that the fact be emphasized, as far as is possible, that the occasion is an audience requested by the artists themselves. The salon in the Borgia apartment might be designated for the purpose (the others are earmarked for the ceremony on the following day). He wishes the Cardinal Secretary of State to be informed of all this.

The undersigned requests instructions: M. Tannstein is waiting as a matter of urgency.

The document, signed with the initials of Giovanni Battista Montini, bears in pencil the words: "notes revised this morning by His Holiness."

In the end, Manager Tietjen was obliged to return to Berlin abruptly. No concert took place; Pius XII simply received a group of musicians in audience.

Only the Vatican Archives can disclose whether the sermons by Msgr. Galen, Bishop of Münster—who, in August 1941, made a public stand against the killing of mental patients and obliged Hitler to put an end to this operation—were delivered on instructions from the Pope or were the result of the Bishop's personal initiative alone. The Wilhelmstrasse Archives gave no indication of any sort on this point.

3. The Political Attitude of the Holy See, Spring 1941

ON FEBRUARY 15, 1941, Ribbentrop wrote to Bergen:

¶ A confidential report reaching me contains the following remark: "On a number of occasions in the recent past the Pope, surprisingly enough, has expressed extreme optimism about Germany's prospects of victory. In conversations with high-ranking members of the Italian nobility, he has left no doubt that everyone in Italy must get used to the idea of certain victory for Germany. Request full report on this by return.[3]

Bergen replied:

¶ Interesting statements by the Pope, which had been dropped in informal discussion after formal receptions . . . or in the course of private audiences . . . have been passed to the Embassy again and again through confidential channels . . . To the extent that a check on each individual instance was feasible, it has been possible to establish that the remarks repeated had been torn from their context or had been considerably modified in the telling, which was less objective than imaginative. Much the same, no doubt, is true in the case of the statements which you have been kind enough to bring to my attention. I do not regard them as being very probable in the form given, not by any means because Pius XII harbors any doubts about our final victory but because, as the supranational, supreme spiritual

[3] Telegram from Ribbentrop to Bergen, Feb. 15, 1941, ibid. (MS).

head of the Catholics of all lands, he displays an almost timid concern to exercise caution and restraint in making statements about the conjectural outcome of the War. . . . Undoubtedly, our tremendous successes in the military field and in foreign affairs have not failed to impress the Pope and his entourage. This is evident from the utterances of personalities particularly close to Pius XII, who describe Germany as the presumptive victor in this struggle, as if this were a foregone conclusion. Here it must be borne in mind that, in the final analysis, the Pope, regardless of the impartiality that is dictated by his position, feels as an Italian feels. On this ground alone, and for purely sentimental reasons, he can never wish for a defeat of the Axis Powers. But there is no doubt whatever that, aside from the Italians, there is no nation to which the Pope's inner feelings bring him closer than to the Germans, a people for whose great qualities his admiration is unconcealed; his objections are purely a matter of Church policy and religious in nature. To stamp him as "Francophile"—as so often happens, even among Germans, through ignorance of the circumstances and their background—is thoroughly misguided.

Notwithstanding Pius XII's sympathy for the Axis Powers, if our opponents were utterly destroyed or the War unduly prolonged, he would view these developments as harboring the danger of further advances by Bolshevism, with its antireligious concomitants.

The efforts of Pius XII have been, and are, therefore, directed at contributing to the earliest possible conclusion of the War, and in this context he probably has at the back of his mind the idea of mediating—if only behind the scenes—at the right time. Obviously, if he were to make injudicious statements in favor of one or another of the parties, he would himself only prejudice any prospect of his playing such a role.[4]

Bergen's report confirms the hypotheses that we have put forward to explain the Pope's attempt at mediation in June 1940: what would particularly disturb Pius XII henceforward was the possibility of a spread of Bolshevism as a consequence of the war. For this reason, he wished to contribute, at the earliest possible moment, to bringing about the cessation of hostilities, in spite of the fact that a peace secured in 1940 or early in 1941 would sanction the hegemony of National-Socialist Germany throughout the European continent.

The Pope's political considerations, clear as they were to Bergen, were less well understood in the United States. On May 24, 1941, German Intelligence sent the following report, written around May 10, to the Wilhelmstrasse:

¶ There is lively concern in Vatican political circles about an exchange of letters between the Holy See and the Archbishop of New York who is empowered, *pro tem,* to act as the connecting link between the Vatican and the American Government while peacemaking efforts are in progress. The Archbishop is demanding of the Vatican that the warring parties be asked to recognize, as a basis for peace proposals, the application of the ethnic principle in the determination of the new frontiers. This is also stated to be the requirement of the American Government as a prelude to common action. The Polish delegation to the Vatican, like the Archbishop, has declared unequivocally that only a clear-cut posture on the part of the Vatican in this matter

---

[4] Telegram from Bergen to Ribbentrop, Feb. 15, 1940, StS: V, AA, Bonn (MS).

can uphold the authority of the Pope among the American and Polish Catholics and dispel certain doubts about the independence of Vatican policy which have arisen from the ambiguous phrasing of all statements made by the Pope concerning the great events that so far have occurred. The strictest secrecy is being observed in the Vatican regarding the correspondence with the Archbishop of New York.[5]

The dilemma confronting the Holy See was obvious. To the Allies, peace was inconceivable unless the independence of Poland and, eventually, Czechoslovakia was restored. What that meant in the present case was respect for ethnographic principles. To the Reich, such conditions were obviously totally unacceptable, and the Pope, out of consideration for Germany, could not allow himself the smallest declaration in this sense. His silence, however, did more and more to injure his moral prestige in the United States and elsewhere and, by virtue of that fact, impaired his chances of mediation.

A strange report concerning relations between the Americans and the Vatican reached German Military Intelligence in July 1941. The report had been drawn up in June, before the beginning of the campaign in Russia, by an agent in contact with the Holy See:

¶ A few weeks ago, Tittmann, the assistant to the American Special Envoy to the Vatican, had several talks with Pope Piux XII. Tittmann complained to the Pope that the Vatican was far too lenient in its attitude to the dictators. He used this opportunity to point to a fact which is almost unknown to the public: Even before the War, the Vatican found itself in constant financial embarrassment. In the meantime, the largest contributors of money—the Nether-

5 Report of Inf. III, No. 139, May 24, 1941, StS: V, AA, Bonn (MS).

lands, Belgium, France, Austria, Spain—have dropped out. Consequently, since the beginning of the War the Vatican has regularly received a considerable sum from the U.S.A. which is described as money collected by American Catholics but which, in reality, is drawn from secret funds held by Roosevelt. Tittmann harped on these donations from the U.S.A. like a banker calling a debtor to account. Disregarding his unusually sharp tone, the Pope answered mildly that most of the money had been utilized to set up a network of confidential informants in a great variety of countries and that people in the U.S.A. must understand the attitude of the Vatican. War between Germany and Russia was imminent and the Vatican would do everything to hasten the outbreak of that War, even to the point of encouraging Hitler with a promise of moral support. Germany, he said, would be victorious against Russia but would be weakened so considerably that it would then be possible to adopt a very different approach toward that country.

The Pope made similar statements to Dr. Papée, the Polish Ambassador to the Vatican, when the latter complained in private audience about the lack of support for Poland on the part of the Vatican. The Pope stressed that Germany, when weakened by war with Russia, could be prevailed upon under pressure to put Poland back on its feet again.[6]

Needless to say, this report must be read with the greatest circumspection.

On June 22, 1941, the Germans launched their offensive against the Soviet Union.

[6] Memorandum of Amt Ausland/Abw. III, July 12, 1941, Pol I M, AA, Bonn (MS).

Chapter IV

GERMANY ATTACKS RUSSIA; THE UNITED STATES ENTERS THE WAR; THE EXTERMINATION OF THE JEWS (FIRST PHASE)

June 1941–December 1941

---

1. Germany Attacks Russia

ON JUNE 24, 1941, Bergen wrote:

¶ According to the statements of leading personages in the office of the Secretary of State, repeated to me by a reliable agent, our march into Russia caused no surprise in the Vatican.

The two following observations are characteristic of the way the news was received in the Vatican:

1. Extension of the War to Russia would contribute considerably to the clearing of the air that is necessary for the new order in Europe. There had been reason to fear that Bolshevism—as a repository of power in Europe, and in-

deed in the world as a whole—would remain intact until the end of the War, or even emerge from it strengthened, while all other social forces were suffering. If Russia were subdued, a considerable weakening of Bolshevist influence in the world, at the very least, would be inevitable.

2. Godless Russia on the side of the "democracies" eliminated their pretext that theirs was "a crusade in the cause of Christianity." On a previous occasion, the Vatican had already rejected such an argument to justify this war.

In quarters close to the Vatican, this new phase of the War is being greeted with a certain amount of relief and is being followed with particular interest.[1]

The Vatican's attitude described by Bergen can scarcely be doubted. It was in conformity with the positions adopted earlier by the Vatican in regard to the Bolshevik danger and it will be confirmed more than once by documents cited hereafter. The negative tone of the Holy See toward the democracies was no more surprising, for these henceforth would be allies (effective, as in the case of Great Britain, or potential, as in the case of the United States) of the Soviet Union. But what position would the Holy See adopt officially?

The Germans were able to congratulate themselves on a manifestation of sympathy by implication. Up to June 22, 1941, the Vatican Radio had frequently mentioned, in more or less veiled terms, the fate of the Church in Poland. In June, Bergen had complained about this to the Pope.[2] From the start of the Russian campaign, all unfavorable references to the

---

[1] Bergen telegram to Berlin, June 24, 1941, StS: V, AA, Bonn (MS).
[2] Letter from Bergen to Berlin, June 22, 1941, *DGFP* (D, XIII), p. 1082.

Reich disappeared from the broadcasts of the Vatican Radio. On June 26, Weizsäcker wrote:

¶ The Nuncio asked me today whether we had had reason to make any new complaints about the Vatican Radio. I answered in the negative as far as the recent past was concerned.[3]

And on July 3:

¶ The Nuncio asked me today whether the Vatican Radio had left any unpleasant impressions with us lately. I replied that I had heard no complaints about the Vatican station recently.[4]

However, the Holy See adopted no clear position in favor of Reich action against Russia.

In a long report dated August 23, Menshausen, the Chargé d'Affaires, analysed the attitude of the Vatican:

¶ In his public statements, the Pope has so far taken no definite stand regarding the war with the Soviet Union. It is a fact, nevertheless, that a passage in his radio address of June 29 (the Feast of Peter and Paul) refers to the fight against Bolshevism. According to the official German translation it runs: "Assuredly, in the darkness of the storm there is no lack of rays of light which uplift the heart with great and holy expectations—high-minded gallantry in defense of the foundations of Christian culture and confident hopes for its triumph . . ." I hear from an informed source that, in saying this, Pius XII meant to express the thought that the toll of sacrifice in this war had not been in vain and was leading, by the will of Providence, to victory over Bolshevism. (Pius XI had made pronouncements of a fundamen-

3 Minute by Weizsäcker, June 26, 1941, StS: V, AA, Bonn (MS).
4 Minute by Weizsäcker, July 3, 1941, ibid. (MS).

tal character against "Bolshevik and atheistic Communism" in his encyclical *Divini Redemptoris* of March 18, 1937.)

As regards public statements from other Vatican sources, the only thing known is one address made at the beginning of this month by Archbishop Constantini, Secretary of the Congregation for the Propagation of the Faith, at a festival service in the Basilica of Concordia (Province of Venice), in which he said, among other things: "Just as yesterday on Spanish soil, so today in Bolshevik Russia itself, in that boundless land where Satan seemed to have found his instruments and his best collaborators among the highest authorities of the Republics—there, brave soldiers of our own fatherland, along with others, are fighting the greatest battle of all. We wish with all our hearts that this battle may bring us the conclusive victory over a Bolshevism bent on negation and upheaval."

At the end, Constantini invoked the blessing of God on the Italian and German soldiers who "at this decisive hour, are defending the ideal of our freedom against Red barbarism."

As to the reasons that have prompted the Vatican to exercise restraint, the article appearing in the issue dated August 2, 1941, of the Fascist periodical *Relazioni Internazionali* under the title "The Holy See faces the U.S.S.R." may provide some enlightenment. This periodical is published, as is well known, by the Institute for the Study of International Politics in Milan and is used from time to time as a mouthpiece by the Italian Ministry of Foreign Affairs. It is widely assumed in Church and diplomatic quarters here that this article was initiated by an authoritative Italian source and written by a personality familiar with Vatican thinking. The content coincides with statements concerning the attitude of the Vatican made to me by an informant close to the Vatican even before the article was published.

The author notes at the outset that since the start of hostilities against the U.S.S.R. the international press has shown intense interest in discovering what attitude the Holy See would adopt. As the military operations proceeded and "an ideal voluntary coalition against the Bolshevik regime" took shape in many countries of Europe, the expectation that the Vatican position would be clarified spread from journalists to political quarters and even to the masses. Expectation had been heightened still further by the official announcement that on the Feast of Peter and Paul the Pope would speak on the radio on "Divine Providence in the Events of Today."

However, the broadcast address on June 29 contained no specific declaratons. Be that as it may, it is pointed out in Vatican circles that the general phrasing of the address reveals "motives and principles" which may throw light on the nature and the causes of the Vatican posture in the fight against Soviet Russia.

This is explained by the "extreme, yet vigilant restraint" which is in keeping with the traditional practice of the Holy See. It is therefore in no way indicative of aloof indifference or of the kind of irresolution that waits for decisive events to happen.

The Roman Catholic Church has already conclusively defined its standpoint not only toward the errors of the Bolshevik "mystique" but also toward the Bolshevik Government and the state which translates the theories into practice. In the encyclical *Divini Redemptoris,* the Pope does not hesitate—and this is an extremely rare case in Church history—to hurl at the regime and at the government a damning verdict that is both explicit and formal:

"We accuse the system, its originators and promoters, who regarded Russia as the most suitable country in which to put into practice a system that had been worked out for decades and who, from there, are tirelessly spreading it all over the world!"

From this it emerges that, as conceived by the Holy See, Bolshevism is regarded as an evil that is not merely endemic but a danger to the whole world; and the first victim of which—as well as the base, as it were, for its future expansion throughout the world—is Russia. From the doctrinal and traditional standpoint of the Catholic Church, as expounded in the encyclical, there is an indisputable conclusion to be drawn. It is that the Holy See is not only gratified to watch the progressive rollback of atheistic Bolshevism but virtually desires and favors this.

In these circumstances (says the writer) no one can fail to see that the reserved and cautious attitude adopted by the Vatican toward the armed action against the U.S.S.R. must be determined by considerations and reasons of vital importance.

Without delving into detail, a precise knowledge of which is the exclusive prerogative of the highest office in the Church, one need only keep in mind the doctrinal requirements and the traditional usages of the Church to identify the main viewpoints which today set the direction of the Vatican attitude toward the war against the U.S.S.R.

It is noted in Vatican quarters that there is widespread talk of a "crusade," and it is certainly true that the spontaneous and unanimous participation of governments and peoples in the armed struggle against Bolshevism may well recall the Catholic movement in the Middle Ages which took up arms against Mohammedanism. But this description has not been echoed in the words of the Pope. Although the fight against Soviet Russia has its ideological—and even its religious—side, the Holy See cannot regard it exclusively from this point of view (as intervention on its part would require), because this factor, however basic, is intimately bound up with others of a more fortuitous nature—military and political interests, above all. Added to this is the fact that the Holy See, however much it might like to see the Bolshevist plague wiped out, could not wish this to happen at the price of military carnage on such a gigantic scale.

The article ends as follows: While the anti-Bolshevik attitude of the Holy See is thus proven beyond question—it is said in the Vatican—it is necessary, on the other hand, to appreciate the special circumstances which have obliged the Holy See to stay on a plane that is entirely spiritual and religious in character.[5]

On September 12, Menshausen completed the report he had sent in August:

¶ As a supplement to my report of the 23rd ultimo (A 479) regarding the attitude of the Vatican to the war against the Soviet Union, I should like to give you a further small sketch of the prevailing mood based on conversations with well informed personalities, some of them in authority:

Apart from the arguments reproduced in the report, which are designed more for public consumption, intelligence available in the Vatican about the state of religious policy in Germany has helped, if it has not played a decisive role, in determining the reserve exercised so far by the Pope toward our battle against Bolshevik Russia. In various high-level Vatican conversations, and in response to questions

[5] Letter from Menshausen to Berlin, Aug. 23, 1941, StS: V, AA Bonn (MS).

as to the reasons for this reserve, it was intimated that after the way things had developed in Germany and in the territories in our hands, there had been reason to fear that, once Bolshevism had been suppressed, the Catholic Church—indeed, Christianity as such—would fall, as it were, out of the frying pan into the fire. If the Pope were now to raise his voice against Bolshevism, against which he had repeatedly expressed himself in principle, he would be obliged also to take a stand against "the anticlerical measures and anti-Christian tendencies in Germany"; information on this subject, which was "constantly coming into" the Vatican supplied "a crushing volume of material" to justify such a step; the Pope's silence was the best proof that he would like to avoid saying anything that would damage Germany.

In a confidential talk, a high-ranking personality, who is familiar with the mood in the Vatican and is close to the Italian Government, described in these terms the reasons for the Pope's reserve in regard to our fight against Bolshevik Russia: when political measures against the Church in the Reich had been visibly intensified, Pius XII had felt that he could no longer be responsible for further silence on the subject.[6] Nevertheless, when the war against Soviet Russia began, he had refrained from taking what was deemed to be the necessary step, in order not to injure Germany or her allies in a phase of events that was so crucial for the fate of the world. To go beyond this and openly take sides in public in the fight against Soviet Russia

[6] The personage quoted by Menshausen was probably alluding to the measures adopted by the Germans against the Church in Poland, part of which (the Warthegau or Wartheland) the Reich had annexed (hence the phrase "measures . . . in the Reich"). The Wilhelmstrasse archives provide no further information about any intention Pius XII might have had, in 1940 or early in 1941, to drop his reserve; on that point, the Vatican archives could enlighten us.

had been made impossible for him by German actions.

In his heart, so runs the constantly reiterated assurance, Pius XII is on the side of the Axis Powers. In this connection, attention is also drawn to the words which he directed at Italy in his last radio address on June 29 this year: "In blessing thee (Rome), We bless the entire Italian nation, which not only has the privilege of enclosing the core of Church unity but combines with this privilege the manifest tokens of its divine mission." Moreover (we are told), there are plenty of indications for the attitude of the Vatican. The speech of such a prominent personage as Archbishop Constantini, Secretary of the Congregation for the Propagation of the Faith (the relevant passages of which were reproduced in the report mentioned above), was of particular significance in this respect because it could not possibly have been made without the consent of the Holy See. The declaration of the Italian clergy and numerous articles appearing in the Catholic press throughout Italy, in which the importance of the fight against Bolshevism is elucidated, can also be traced to directives given by the Vatican or by Catholic Action.[7]

Menshausen's second report seems to offer a rather plausible description of the attitude adopted by Pius XII. That the Pope wished for a victory of the Reich over Russia is possible; that it was impossible for him to take up a position openly in favor of a Germany which was persecuting the Church is no less evident, particularly if account is taken of the reactions which such a stand would have provoked among all Catholics, both in the occupied countries and in the United States.

[7] Letter from Menshausen to Weizsäcker, Sept. 12, 1941, StS: V, AA, Bonn (MS).

Two documents based on testimony from a Spanish source confirm the Pope's attitude toward the German attack on Russia. On October 4, 1941, Weizsäcker wrote:

¶ The Spanish Ambassador, who has just returned here from Madrid, conveyed to me on behalf of Serrano Suñer the content of two identical conversations which were conducted by the Nuncio in Madrid and by the Nuncio in Vichy with the Spanish Ambassador there—obviously, therefore, under instructions. The two representatives of the Curia stated that it had been reported to the Pope that the Führer had told Franco in Hendaye that the Pope was an enemy of the Führer. If, they said, such words had been used or, worse, if they reflected the Führer's view, then the Pope regretted this. Pius XII had friendly feelings for the Reich. He had no more ardent wish for the Führer than to see him gain a victory over Bolshevism. Once Soviet Russia had been decisively defeated, the moment would perhaps have come for peace to be proclaimed. The Pope would particularly deplore it if, after such an achievement on the part of the Führer and the Third Reich, such inaccurate notions of his feelings should prevail among us in Germany. Suñer replied at once to the Nuncio in Madrid that the information that had been passed to the Pope was false. On the contrary, the Führer had told Franco that he attached importance to a good relationship with the Curia as he himself housed some 30 million Catholics within the boundaries of the Reich . . .[8]

The second document, dated November 17, complements the preceding one. Bergen wrote to the Wilhelmstrasse:

[8] Memorandum by Weizsäcker, Oct. 4, 1941, ibid., (MS).

¶ Yanguas Messia, Spanish Ambassador to the Holy See, who has returned from a four-month leave in Spain, has been received in private audience by the Pope in the past few days. He told me that, on instructions from Franco, he had informed Pius XII that the information conveyed to the Pope to the effect that the Führer had told the Caudillo at Hendaye that Pius XII was an enemy of the Führer was incorrect. Pope replied that he was sincerely pleased to receive this information because he had always felt, and still felt, not only the warmest sympathy for Germany but also admiration for the great qualities of the Führer.[9]

2. The United States Enters the War

DESPITE the official reserve maintained by the Holy See in the face of the German attack on Russia, German reports suggested that American Catholics were becoming increasingly critical of Pius XII because of an attitude on his part which looked like complicity with the Axis Powers. On July 18, 1941, the German Secret Service passed the following information to the Wilhelmstrasse:

¶ . . . In the Vatican, the unpleasant polemic between Secretary of State Maglione and the Catholic Archbishop of New York . . . is still a carefully guarded secret. In one of his letters to the Vatican, the Archbishop used phrases to the effect, among other things, that in view of the Pope's ambiguous statements about the responsibility of one or

[9] Telegram from Bergen to Berlin, Nov. 17, 1941, ibid. In a letter sent to the Italian weekly *Gente* on March 24, 1965, former Ambassador José de Yanguas Messia writes that he remembers his conversation, that the Pope mentioned his warm sympathy for Germany but did not say anything about his great admiration for the Führer. It is difficult to assess how precise the memory of the former ambassador is after twenty-four years.

the other of the belligerents his prestige in America was declining and that the American Catholics had no confidence in the Pope's opinion on account of his Italian origin. It was suspected there, not without reason, that in spite of everything the Pope sympathized with Italy's imperialist endeavors and because of this he could not maintain his authority as the spiritual father of the Catholic Church among the masses of the faithful in the United States. The Secretary of State answered that he could not even show the Pope this offensive letter and that the Archbishop must not only believe in the sanctity of the Pope's opinion but also must defend his authority in the eyes of American Catholics. The Pope is alleged to be adopting a quite clear attitude in the quarrel between the two disputing parties. He condemns the attack by Germany but, at the same time, expresses disapproval of England and France which, though wealthy nations, were unwilling to relinquish part of the colonial riches they had accidentally acquired to the impoverished peoples of Germany and Italy . . . The deterioration in the relations between Vatican City and the American Catholics can no longer be concealed.[1]

In September, Myron Taylor, President Roosevelt's Special Envoy to the Holy See, arrived at the Vatican on a brief mission and had a number of talks with the Pope. The German diplomats at the Holy See admitted that they were only partially informed about these conversations. Menshausen thought that the President of the United States had renewed his efforts to induce the Holy See to take a stand opposed to Hitler on the war and had tried at the same time to justify

[1] Inf. III of July 18, 1941, StS: V, AA, Bonn (MS).

the material aid that was being given by the United States to the Soviet Union by stressing that the latter had just restored religious liberty.[2]

On September 30, the German Ambassador in Madrid wrote to Berlin that the Japanese Ambassador in the Spanish capital had informed him of the content of the talks between the Pope and Taylor and had told him that he possessed documentary proof of his information:

¶ . . . On Myron Taylor's first mission to Rome, Taylor, acting on instructions from Roosevelt, expounded to the Pope the argument that, as regards the nonextension of the war and the restoration of peace, the interests of the U.S.A. and the Holy See were parallel. The Pope replied, in a note of January 7, 1940, that he was of the same opinion and that if the war did spread, the cause of faith and civilization might be lost.

This time Myron Taylor had instructions from Roosevelt to make clear to the Pope why the U.S.A. had found itself compelled to adopt a posture that was at least analogous to belligerency and to take part in the conflict. The Pope is said to have shown no great understanding of this and to have emphasized again that extension of the war would be the greatest of all calamities; he was glad (he said) that, in spite of this, the U.S.A. was still neutral to all because this was the only way in which it could cooperate with the Holy See for the restoration of peace.

The Japanese Ambassador stressed repeatedly that this information was absolutely reliable.[3]

[2] Telegram from Menshausen to Berlin, Sept. 12, 1941, ibid. (MS).
[3] Telegram from Stohrer to Berlin, Sept. 30, 1941, StS: V, AA, Bonn (MS).

On December 7, 1941, the Japanese attacked Pearl Harbor and the United States was drawn into the war. On the 11th, Bergen wrote to Berlin:

¶ In authoritative Vatican circles, Roosevelt's behavior is criticized with unconcealed severity. The President (it is said) had not only made no effort to prevent the war from spreading to other countries but had finally maneuvered his own country into the war. This action was all the more reprehensible because he had established contact with the Vatican at Christmas 1939 on the basis of a program which, according to his own statements, was aimed precisely at preventing the war from spreading and at promoting possibilities of peace in every way.[4]

On December 15, Bergen sent an even more detailed report:

¶ The verdict on Roosevelt in the Vatican is becoming sharper and sharper in tone . . . The judgment of an authoritative Vatican source is clearly to the effect that Roosevelt has lacked sincerity from the beginning and that he has played a double game.

It is likely that the report made by Galeazzi, Director General of the Vatican Economic Service and one of the Pope's closest confidants, about his impressions of his recent stay in the United States . . . contributed to this judgment. I am reliably informed that Galeazzi, who had maintained good relations with leading American personages, has made very disparaging statements about conditions there. In spite of the incitement in high places against the Axis Powers, he found the country as unprepared for war as it could possibly be. He got the impression that the

[4] Telegram from Bergen to Berlin, Dec. 11, 1941, ibid.

strikes in important branches of industry amounted virtually to sabotage of Roosevelt's policy. The utter lack of
discipline which he observed in every field of activity, even
in the deportment of the individual American—as contrasted with the seriousness with which the Englishmen he
met on his journey are facing the [. . .] of the War—had
struck him as particularly blatant.[5]

The Vatican's attitude regarding the entry of the United
States into the war had a sequel which is not without interest.
At the Rio de Janeiro Conference in January 1942, Washington made great efforts to persuade all the South-American
republics to break off diplomatic relations with the Axis and
with Japan. The United States' action did not achieve complete success. On March 21, 1942, Bergen conveyed the following information on the subject to the Wilhelmstrasse:

¶ I learn through secret channels that Holy See, apparently
at the instance of Italian Government, did, in fact, use its
diplomatic representative to lobby the countries taking part
in the Conference of Rio de Janeiro, before Conference
convened, with object of ensuring their continued neutrality. However, he felt compelled by the United Press report
to issue denial through Apostolic Delegate in Washington
in order to avoid charge of intervention or partisanship.[6]

3. The Anti-Jewish Legislation; the Concentration and Extermination of the Jews (First Phase)

ON THE NIGHT of November 9 to 10, 1938, the Nazis, to
"avenge" the assassination of the German Counselor of Em-

---

[5] Telegram from Bergen to Berlin, Dec. 15, 1941, ibid.
[6] Telegram from Bergen to Berlin, March 21, 1942, ibid. (MS).

bassy vom Rath by Hershel Grynzpan, a young Polish Jew, killed several dozen Jews, incarcerated more than 20,000 of them in concentration camps and set fire to nearly 200 synagogues. This was the notorious *Kristallnacht.* Throughout the length and breadth of the Greater German Reich, *the voice of one single priest was raised in protest,* that of Bernhard Lichtenberg, Provost of St. Hedwig's Cathedral in Berlin:

¶ What happened here yesterday, we know; what will happen tomorrow, we do not know; but we are witnesses of what is happening today. Outside (this Church), a synagogue is burning—and a synagogue too, is a house of God.[7]

From the moment Hitler took power, numerous German ecclesiastics had associated themselves with the anti-Semitic measures of the new regime, sometimes lending them active support.[8] The racial laws were accepted by the episcopate of the Reich and, in 1935, Archbishop Gröber of Freiburg was able to write:

¶ Every people bears responsibility for the success of its existence, and the absorption of entirely alien blood will always constitute a risk for a nation which has proved its historic worth. Consequently, the right to safeguard the purity of the race, and to devise measures necessary to that end, can be denied to no one. The Christian religion simply demands that the means used shall not be contrary to moral law and natural justice.[9]

When, less than two years after the outbreak of war, the first important measures were taken against the Jews in the

[7] Alfons Erb: *Bernhard Lichtenberg: Domprobst von St. Hedwig zu Berlin* (Berlin: Morus Verlag; 1949), p. 43.
[8] Lewy: op. cit., Ch. X.
[9] Ibid., p. 275.

Western countries subjected, directly or indirectly, to German authority, the attitude of the Catholic clergy varied considerably from country to country and even from diocese to diocese.

In France, various measures had been directed against the Jews in the Occupied Zone as early as 1940; the discriminatory legislation became systematic when, on March 29, 1941, the Government of Marshal Pétain nominated Xavier Vallat as Commissioner for Jewish Affairs. On July 22, the Vichy Government decreed the "Aryanization" of Jewish enterprises and the control of all funds belonging to Jews.

On July 31, Rabbi Jacob Kaplan, assistant to Chief Rabbi Isaiah Schwartz, addressed to Vallat a letter in which he tried to demonstrate that the measures taken against the Jews were contrary to the injunctions of Christianity. Were not Jesus and his apostles Jews, asked the Rabbi? Rabbi Kaplan's letter appears to have caused some embarrassment in the inner councils of the Vichy Government, as is indicated by the very cautious reply sent by Jarnieu, Vallat's *chef de cabinet*.[1] Consequently, on August 7, Marshal Pétain asked Léon Bérard, his Ambassador to the Holy See, to enquire about the attitude of the Vatican in this matter.

The Ambassador replied on September 2. We shall depart from our normal procedure in this case and quote only those paragraphs of the text which are most directly relevant to our subject. The text has, in fact, been published.[2]

A. *The Church and Racism*

¶ There is a fundamental, unshakable antithesis between Church doctrines and "racist" theories. The Church, which

[1] See on this subject Raul Hilberg: *The Destruction of the European Jews* (Chicago: Quadrangle Books; 1961), pp. 398 f.
[2] Nobécourt, op. cit., appendices.

is by definition universal, preaches the unity of the human race. One and the same Redeemer died for all men; the Gospel was addressed to, and will be proclaimed to, "all creatures." Every human being has an immortal soul which is upheld by the same grace and is summoned to the same salvation as all other souls. This is the medium by which a human being is established in dignity; this is the foundation of his rights, of which his duties are the measure. All these propositions are incompatible with an outlook which derives from the shape of the skull and the nature of the blood the aptitudes and vocations of peoples, their very religion itself, and finally sets up a hierarchy of races, at the apex of which appears a pure or royal race called "Aryan."

In his encyclical *"Mit brennender Sorge"* of March 14, 1937, on National Socialism and the situation of Catholicism in Germany, Pius XI writes: "Whoever takes the race or the people, or the state or the form of the state, or the repositories of power, or any other fundamental value of the human community—all things which occupy a necessary and honorable place in the earthly order—whoever takes these notions and removes them from this scale of values, not excluding even religious values, and defies them through an idolatrous cult, inverts and falsifies the order of things as created and ordained by God. Such a man is far removed from true belief in God and from a conception of life in keeping with that faith . . .

. . . The Church, then, has condemned racism, just as it has condemned Communism.

It cannot, however, be inferred from these teachings regarding racial ideas—far from it—that the Church necessarily condemns every particular measure taken by any state against what is called the Jewish race. Its thought on this matter embraces distinctions and nuances which should be noted. The subject has to be handled differently from case to case.

B. *The Church, the Jewish Problem and Anti-Semitism*

One would seek in vain to extract from canon law, from theology and from pontifical acts a corpus of precepts resembling legislation on Judaism and the Judaic religion. It would not even be easy to find in such sources a body of doctrine with well defined contours.

The principle that emerges first, and appears most certain, is that in the eyes of the Church a Jew who has received valid baptism ceases to be a Jew and merges with "Christ's flock." However, one must not hasten to conclude from this that, to the Church, religion is the only thing that distinguishes Israel among the nations. It does not consider at all that the Jews constitute a simple "spiritual family," like those formed among us, for example, by Catholics and "reformed" Christians. It recognizes that among the distinctive traits of the Israelite community there are peculiarities which are not *racial* but *ethnic*. This it has long since realized and has always taken into account.

We know from general history that the Church has often protected Jews against the violence and injustice of their persecutors and that it has, at the same time, relegated them to ghettos. One of its greatest teachers, St. Thomas Aquinas, has left doctrines interpreting this attitude. He deals with the Jewish question—incidentally, but in very clear terms—in the *Summa Theologiae,* Question 10 of 11a, Hae. art. 9, 10, 11 and 12. This is a summary of his doctrine: tolerance must be shown to the Jews in the exercise

[94]

of their religion; they should be sheltered from religious constraints; their children should not be forcibly baptized without the consent of the parents. On the other hand, while proscribing all oppressive policies toward the Jews, St. Thomas nevertheless recommends that appropriate measures be taken to limit their action in society and to restrict their influence. It would be contrary to reason to allow them to exercise the powers of government in a Christian state and, by so doing, subject Catholics to their authority. Consequently, it is legitimate to deny them access to functions in the public arena and equally legitimate to admit them only by fixed quotas to universities (*numerus clausus*) and to the liberal professions.

C. *Difficulties between the Holy See and Italy in the Matter of Fascist Legislation Concerning the Jews*

Not only were the measures adopted by the Fascist Government not preceded by negotiations nor by an agreement of any kind between the Holy See and that Government, but they gave rise to serious criticism on the part of the papal authority. It is a matter of great importance to define precisely the nature and the object of that divergence . . .

. . . Fascist law concerning the Jews contains provisions which impinge on the juridical rules of conjugal union. In certain conditions, it prohibits marriage between "Aryan" Italians and persons of the Jewish race, even if they have adopted the Catholic religion. The Church, on its part, considers as valid not only unions between Catholics and converted or baptized Jews but also unions celebrated by canonical rite between Catholics and non-converted Jews, provided that, in the second case, permission in the form of a "dispensation" has been obtained from the Catholic authority. The innovation thus introduced into Italian legislation would have earned, of itself, the disapproval of the papal power. The latter, by reason of one of its oldest and firmest traditions, considers that marriage is essentially a sacrament; as such, stems from the spiritual order at the highest level; and that, in consequence, everything relating to the formation and validity of the matrimonial tie must be regulated by Catholic religious law.

But there was another and, in practical terms, more decisive reason why the new Fascist law met with an unfavorable reception in the Vatican. By enacting statutes, as it had, on marriages between Aryans and non-Aryans, the Fascist state had infringed the Concordat concluded between the Holy See and Italy on February 11, 1939. Article 24 of that convention provided that: "The Italian State, wishing to restore to the institution of marriage—which is the basis of family life—a dignity in keeping with the Catholic traditions of its people, recognizes the marriage sacrament, regulated by canon law, as having civil effects."

. . . It is quite clear that in adhering to this contract, which bears the signature of Signor Mussolini, the Italian State renounced the "secularization" of marriage . . .

D. *What Contradictions Are There Between Catholic Doctrine and the French Law of June 2, 1941, Concerning the Status of Jews?*

To achieve greater simplicity and clarity, it is appropriate, I believe, to consider that law first from the point of view of its real object and its practical scope, i.e. in the light of those of its provisions which contain interdictions, inhibitions, and prohibitions in regard to Jews. Unless they are in a position to be able to claim the benefit of qualifying clauses provided for in the text, Jews are excluded from a large number of public functions. Furthermore, they are forbidden to practise certain restricted professions, which are enumerated, and they will not be admitted to certain other professions except in accordance with quotas and limitations to be determined by decree.

In principle, there is nothing in these measures which the Holy See would find to criticize. The Vatican considers that a state applying such rules is making legitimate use of its power, and that the spiritual power should not interfere in the internal policy of states in such matters. Moreover, the Church has never professed that the same rights should be accorded to all citizens or recognized as theirs. It has never ceased to proclaim the dignity of, and respect for, the human person. But one may be sure that it does not interpret such things rigorously, in the same way as do the spiritual heirs of Rousseau and Condorcet. To judge this, it is sufficient to bear in mind all that separates the dogma of original sin from the teachings bequeathed to us by those philosophers: the natural goodness of man; the unlimited capacity of the human mind for progress; the individualist conception of law; and social and political organization.

It follows that the law of June 2, 1941 sets out from a juridical definition of the Jew in which the legislator refers expressly to the notion of "race." Again, it should be noted that if one compares this law of June 2 with that of October 3, which it abrogated and replaced, one finds that the new text has reduced the place and the role assigned to the idea of "race." If a Jew proves that he belonged before June 25, 1940 to the Catholic confession or to the Lutheran or Calvinist confession, he ceases to be "regarded as a Jew," provided, further, that he does not have more than two grandparents of Jewish race. In this case, then, the law attaches juridical effects to "conversion." The fact remains that an Israelite, though duly converted and baptized, will be considered a Jew if he is the issue of at least three grandparents of Jewish race, i.e., who have belonged to the Judaic religion.

In that, it must be recognized, there is a contradiction between French law and the doctrine of the Church.

E. *Practical Consequences of this Contradiction. Conclusion.*

I have indicated the only point on which the law of June 2, 1941 is at odds with a principle professed by the Roman Church. It does not follow at all from this doctrinal divergence that the French State is threatened, I will not say by a conflict like that which has arisen between the Holy See and the Fascist Government, but even by censure or disapproval which the Holy See might come to express in one form or another with regard to the statute on the Jews.

. . . As I have been told by an authorized person at the Vatican, no quarrel will be started with us because of the statute on the Jews. However, a twofold plea has been expressed to me by representatives of the Holy See, with the visible wish to have both submitted to the French Chief of State:

1. That no provision affecting marriage be added to the law concerning the Jews. If we did so, we should run into difficulties of a religious order. Much feeling was stirred up in the Vatican by the fact that Romania adopted, on this capital point, rules of law inspired by, or imitated from, Fascist legislation.

2. That, in the application of the law, the precepts of

[98]

justice and charity be taken into account. Those with whom I talked appeared to me to have in mind above all the liquidation of business in which the Jews hold interest . . .

The analysis of the Vatican's attitude in regard to the discriminatory legislation applied to the Jews, as presented by Léon Bérard, must be read with great caution. Of course, it must be said that a number of dignitaries of the Church were not able to escape the temptation of anti-Semitism; but Bérard's hint that in 1941 the Holy See had given a sort of blanket approval for anti-Semitic measures, provided that they were mitigated by charity, seems difficult to prove.

Léon Bérard does not quote the name of the Vatican personage who is supposed to have affirmed to him that the Holy See had no objection to the statute on the Jews devised by Vichy. This omission is all the more strange because mention of the name of a high dignitary of the Church probably would have had more effect in appeasing the Marshal's conscience than the theological analysis in which the Ambassador indulged.

With these reservations, it must nevertheless be admitted that the last paragraphs of the Bérard report provide a significant insight into the attitude of the Holy See concerning the discriminatory legislation.

At the very moment when Bérard conveyed to Vichy the details of what he believed to be the attitude of the Holy See regarding the French Government's anti-Jewish legislation, the German Special Commandos went into action against the Jewish population in the areas of Russia occupied by the forces of the Reich. In the autumn of 1941, more than half a million Jews were massacred. At the same time, concentration of more than two million Jews in the ghettos of Poland was completed. All was ready for the "final solution."

How much, exactly, was known in the autumn of 1941 of what was happening in the East? No document reveals this. The most that can be said is that the Vatican knew that Jews were being deported toward Eastern Europe because the matter seems to have achieved public notoriety, as is indicated by the attitude of Msgr. Lichtenberg which we shall now describe. But it can not be asserted that the Holy See or Lichtenberg knew more at that time.

On November 11, 1941, Counselor Haidlen sent the following note to Weizsäcker:

¶ With regard to the arrest of Provost Lichtenberg, the official of the Secret State Police (Gestapo) in charge of the case sends the following communication:

"Lichtenberg is stated to have prayed repeatedly for the Jews during the public vespers, and not only for the baptized Jews but also for the prisoners in concentration camps and 'for the millions of people who have been made homeless by the war.' He acknowledged at the same time that he was opposed on principle to National Socialism and declared that he wished to share the fate of the Jews deported to the East so that he could pray for them there."[3]

An unsigned, undated memorandum, probably written by Woermann, follows Haidlen's in the State Secretary's file. It runs as follows:

¶ It is possible that the Nuncio may raise the matter of the arrest of Lichtenberg, Provost of St. Hedwig's Cathedral here. The reason given for the arrest is that when the last

[3] Memorandum from Haidlen to Weizsäcker, Nov. 11, 1941, StS: V, AA, Bonn (MS).

group of Jews was being deported Lichtenberg said a prayer for the Jews.[4]

This memorandum is noteworthy. Its author, anticipating a question from the Nuncio on the subject of Lichtenberg's arrest, made no effort to offer an excuse in general terms, such as "displayed sentiments hostile to the regime" or "causing a breach of the peace," but suggested that Msgr. Orsenigo be told simply, as a matter of course, that Lichtenberg had been arrested because he had prayed for the Jews. The Germans apparently thought that such a reply would be sufficient for Msgr. Orsenigo and, accordingly, for the Pope himself.

In actual fact, Msgr. Orsenigo never inquired about the reasons for Lichtenberg's arrest. He contented himself, at a later date, with requesting that the proceedings in progress against Lichtenberg be speeded up because the imprisoned priest was in a poor state of health.[5] Lichtenberg met his death on the way to Dachau.

At the beginning of December, the news was broadcast from London that the Nuncio in Berlin had received instructions to intervene with the Germans regarding the cruelties committed against prisoners in the concentration camps. Bergen was able to deny this report:

¶ When the London broadcast about the alleged instructions to Berlin Nuncio regarding Polish concentration camps was brought to the notice of Msgr. Domenico Tardini, Undersecretary of State, he described the reports as inaccurate.[6]

---

[4] Memorandum without a signature or date, ibid. (MS).
[5] Memorandum by Weizsäcker of March 10, 1942, ibid. (MS).
[6] Telegram from Bergen to Berlin, Dec. 18, 1941, ibid. (MS).

4. The Shooting of Hostages

ON DECEMBER 5, Weizsäcker had had the following conversation with Msgr. Orsenigo:

¶ Today, the Nuncio cautiously broached the familiar topic of hostages with me to ascertain whether a talk between him and me on the question of the shooting of hostages—latterly in Serbia—would serve any useful purpose. I replied to the Nuncio that, of all the foreign missions which had concerned themselves with the question, the Curia had taken the wisest course by following the fleeting hint I had given to Counselor Colli [an official in the Nuncio's office] at a social meeting and refraining from any further move. Should the Curia feel impelled, in spite of this, to raise the matter again, I should be obliged to give the Nuncio the same answer as Haiti, Mexico and others had received.

The Nuncio fully appreciated this, pointing out that he had not touched on the subject at all and did not wish to. He was also quite clear in his mind that the foreign states who now showed an inclination to intervene had not felt any injury to their humanitarian consciences when démarches of the same kind were called for by action on the part of our opponents.[7]

[7] Memorandum by Weizsäcker, Dec. 5, 1941, ibid. (MS).

Chapter V

"THE FINAL SOLUTION"

January 1942–Early 1943

IN JANUARY 1942, the Germans decided on a "final solution" to the Jewish problem, that is, the extermination of all the Jews in the regions under their control.[1] The protocol of the Wannsee Conference stated that the final solution of the Jewish problem would have to be applied to some 11 million persons.

1. Information Reaching the Holy See Early in 1942

WHAT, exactly, did the Holy See know about the extermination of the Jews from the beginning of 1942? That is one of the basic questions which I should have liked to answer in this study. The fact is that the documents at our disposal do not yet allow us to go beyond the stage of conjecture. Here, too, we can only hope that the Vatican archives will soon make it possible for the researcher to arrive at a definite answer.

---

[1] This chapter is based mainly on material from the Zionist Archives and American documents, as well as from important German documents.

Two interesting documents suggest that the Holy See may have suspected something quite early in 1942.

Hans Gmelin, a member of the German Legation at Bratislava, stated under oath in June 1948 that the Apostolic Nuncio wrote in February 1942, in two notes delivered to Msgr. Tuka, the Slovak Premier, that it was incorrect to believe that the Jews were being sent to Poland to work; in reality, they were being exterminated there.[2]

On February 9, Weizsäcker wrote the following note on a talk with Nuncio Orsenigo:

¶ The Nuncio then asked that consideration be given nevertheless to the possibility of moving the Catholic priests in the Auschwitz concentration camp to Dachau. For him, as representative of the Curia (he said), this was certainly a modest request.[3]

The reason behind this request may have been that the Nuncio had certain information at his disposal concerning the difference between a "concentration camp" (Dachau) and an "extermination camp" (Auschwitz).

2. *The Intervention of the Jewish Organizations*

On March 17, 1942, representatives of the Jewish Agency, the World Jewish Congress and the Swiss Israelite community, after an interview with Msgr. Bernardini, the Apostolic Nuncio in Berne, forwarded to him the following letter and *aide-mémoire:*

[2] Affidavit by Hans Gmelin, June 15, 1948, in "United States Military Tribunals against Ernst von Weizsäcker *et al.*" (mimeographed), Nuremberg Document NG-5291.
[3] Memorandum by Weizsäcker, Feb. 9, 1942, StS: V, AA, Bonn (MS).

¶ Your Excellency:

Further to the audience which Your Excellency was kind enough to grant us yesterday, we beg leave to send you enclosed, in accordance with your request, two copies of a brief memorandum on the situation of the Jews in the countries of Central and Eastern Europe.

We take the liberty of drawing attention very particularly to the cases of Slovakia, Croatia, Hungary and Unoccupied France, where measures already taken or in progress can perhaps still be rescinded or at least alleviated by the intervention of the Holy See, as we were bold enough to suggest to Your Excellency.

We take this opportunity of expressing to you our profound gratitude for the benevolent and understanding reception that you were kind enough to give the delegation from the Jewish organizations which had the privilege of approaching you yesterday.

Assuring Your Excellency of our respectful esteem, we remain, etc.[4]

1. The multiplicity of measures, dictated by violent anti-Semitism, which have been taken in the past few years against the Jews living in Germany and the territories annexed to Germany are more or less well known to public opinion. They consist in the absolute exclusion of Jews from all professions, all trades and all economic activity in general, except for incorporation in the system of forced labor adopted to meet the needs of war. They consist also in the confiscation of almost all the Jews' worldly goods and, in countless cases, of persecution in various forms, such as arrest, internment in concentration camps or mass expulsion

---

[4] Letter from Lichtheim and Riegner to Bernardini of March 18, 1942, Zionist Archives, Jerusalem (MS).

of Jews—stripped in advance of all they possess—either to Poland or to concentration camps in France. Through the forced emigration which was pursued up to the outbreak of war and by reason of the privation and persecution they have endured, the number of German and Austrian Jews has fallen from around 800,000 to about 200,000.

The remainder of the Jewish population in what was once Czechoslovakia, now living in the *"Protectorate of Bohemia-Moravia"* and numbering some 70,000, have been the victims, since the country was occupied, of similar measures, and are at this moment on the point of being concentrated *en bloc* in a ghetto established at Theresienstadt.

2. Analogous measures, less rigorous in certain cases but even more rigorous in others, have fallen upon the Jews in all the countries occupied during the war by the German Army, such as Belgium, Holland, the Occupied Zone of France, Yugoslavia, Greece, the Baltic countries and notably Poland, where concentration of masses of Jews in ghettos surrounded by unscalable walls has created indescribable misery and caused epidemics which, at this moment, are literally decimating these populations.

3. Germany's allies, imitating the example set by the Reich, have followed the same course and introduced anti-Semitic legislation, or launched violent persecution, aimed at the total dispossession or even the physical extermination of the Jews. This is notably the case in Romania, in the newly created states of Croatia and Slovakia and, to a certain degree too, in Hungary, where preparations are now afoot to incorporate all Jews from 18 to 50 in forced labor units.

4. Among the most striking illustrations of such persecution, we would quote the following:

a) The establishment in Occupied France of reprisal camps at Drancy and Compiègne, near Paris, where approximately 6,000 to 7,000 Jews, who were arrested in the streets or in their own homes in August last, are literally dying of hunger and being used by the military authorities as hostages:

b) The establishment of concentration camps in Unoccupied France; for example, at Gurs, at Récébédou, at Noé, Vernet, Rivesaltes, etc., where several tens of thousands of Jews of all nationalities, who were already living in France or took refuge in France in consequence of the advance of the German armies into Belgium, have been herded—the women and children separated from their husbands and fathers—into sordid huts surrounded by barbed wire, where they have been vegetating for more than two years in unimaginable misery. To these camps, Germany has also sent 9,000 German Jews who had been established for centuries in Baden and the Palatinate.

Apart from these camps, there are also "foreign workers' units" and "social reclassification centers" which are being used under various labels for the purpose of employing on forced labor a group of Jews, many of whom served under the French colors during the war.

c) Among the cruelties perpetrated in the occupied countries by Germany, we would cite the example of several hundred young Dutch Jews who, without any charges' being levelled against them, were sent to the concentration camps at Buchenwald in Germany and Mauthausen in Austria, where virtually all of them perished within a few weeks.

d) Apart from the slow and steady extermination associated with the ghetto system throughout Poland, thousands of Jews in Poland and in the parts of Russia occupied by Germany have been executed by German troops.

e) Eighteen thousand Jews located in Hungary (a number of whom were Hungarian Jews, the others Jews of different nationalities) have been expelled by order of the government and transported in revolting conditions to Eastern Galicia, where they were delivered into the hands of the German authorities, who shot them all, with few exceptions.

f) Early last year, at the time of the Iron Guard uprising in Romania, several thousand Jews were massacred in the streets of Romanian localities. In Bucharest alone, nearly 2,000 persons—intellectuals, officials of Jewish institutions, merchants and industrialists of repute—were killed. Revolting scenes were enacted, notably at the abattoir in Bucharest, to which the Iron Guard dragged the Jews and there slaughtered them like cattle.

g) Most of the Jews in Bucovina, numbering 170,000, were forced to leave their homes and were transported, at the beginning of winter, in open freight cars to Russia. By the time they reached the Russian frontier, a quarter of them were already dead. The survivors were marched for six days toward Mogilev. Those who were in no condition to march were shot.

h) During the reoccupation of Bessarabia by German and Romanian troops, 92,000 Jews were executed by firing squads. A trustworthy report on this subject says that in every town or village Jews were assembled in one place—men, women, children, the aged, the sick, even hospital patients—and, having been tortured and starved for several days, were shot. Among the victims was the Chief Rabbi of Kishinev.

i) In Croatia—where, after the dismemberment of Yugoslavia, there were 30,000 Jews—several thousand families were either deported to desert islands on the Dalmatian coast or incarcerated in concentration camps. After a while, all the *male* Jews in Croatia (as happened in Serbia under German occupation) were sent to labor camps where they were assigned to drainage or sanitation work and where they perished in great numbers as a result of inhuman treatment or through lack of food and clothing. The Croatian Government has not even allowed relief parcels to be sent to them, and it is almost impossible to establish contact with the internees. At the same time, their wives and children were sent to another camp where they, too, are enduring dire privations.

j) In Slovakia, anti-Semitic legislation was promulgated in the course of last year which, like the German legislation, regulates every detail of Jewish life. At the beginning of this month, grave anti-Semitic disturbances broke out. At the same time the government promulgated new decrees aiming at "concentration" of the whole Jewish population of Slovakia, amounting to 90,000 souls. According to reports received in the last few days, this concentration is to be effected as follows: every Jew is authorized to bring a suit, one shirt, and a pair of shoes, all his other property being confiscated by the Hlinka Guard. Preparations have been made to send the Jewish population into camps or ghettos near the Polish frontier between now and March 23. It is feared that they will be sent from there into Poland itself where they will suffer the same fate as the masses of Jews expelled from Romania.

5. It should be noted that among the Hungarian, Romanian and Slovakian Jews, there are several hundred families who are in possession of immigration visas for Palestine or some of the American countries. Above and beyond the steps that can be taken to secure general alleviation of the fate of persecuted and threatened Jewish populations, it is likewise a matter of great urgency to attempt approaches to the competent authorities, notably (for those emigrating to America) to the Italian Government, with a view to obtaining transit visas or, eventually, arranging specially organized convoys to enable the emigrants to reach their ports of embarkation.[5]

This document, which was undoubtedly transmitted by Msgr. Bernardini to the Vatican, could not have failed to confirm information coming from other sources, as was intimated at the beginning of this chapter. The Holy See realized, perhaps, that the Germans had undertaken an operation which would be extended rapidly to all the countries under their control. What would the Vatican's reaction be? In 1942, aside from the intervention by the Nuncio in Slovakia, the German documents record an intervention by the Apostolic Nuncio in France with the government of Marshal Pétain and interventions by Msgr. Orsenigo, the nature of which we shall describe later.

3. The Deportation of the French Jews

THE DEPORTATION of the French Jews began in July 1942. A single document suffices to provide a fairly precise

[5] Ibid. (MS).

picture of the situation. On July 6, 1942, S.S.-Hauptsturm-
führer Dannecker sent the following report to the Reichs-
sicherheitshauptamt (Central Reich Security Office):

¶ Negotiations with the French Government have now had
the following result:

All stateless Jews in the Occupied and Unoccupied Zones
will be made ready for deportation. [The German expression, *Abschub*, literally "to be shoved off," is untranslatably
brutal. Translator's note.]

Premier Laval has proposed that, when Jewish families
are deported from the Unoccupied Zone, children under
sixteen be taken with them. The question of Jewish children left in the Occupied Zone does not interest him . . .

In conclusion, it should be noted that in order to get the
action moving, discussions so far have related only to stateless Jews and/or Jews from foreign states. In the second
phase, Jews naturalized in France after 1919 or after 1927
will be dealt with.[6]

It was at this point that the Holy See intervened with
the government of Marshal Pétain through the medium of
the Nuncio, Msgr. Valerio Valeri, to secure alleviation of the
measures contemplated. On August 18, 1942, Bergen wrote:

¶ I hear very confidentially that the Holy See has approached
the Vichy Government through the medium of the Nuncio
to secure alleviation of the measures taken against Jews in
France. In doing so, Vatican has met a wish conveyed to
it from many quarters. However, no more far-reaching importance should be attached to this step (it is said) than

[6] Document reproduced in Joseph Billig: *Le Commissariat général aux
Questions Juives* (Paris: Éditions du Centre; 1955), Vol. I, pp. 371 f.
Also cited in Léon Poliakov: *Le IIIe Reich et les juifs* (Paris: Galli-
mard; 1959), p. 325.

to other, similar steps which the Vatican has taken for humanitarian reasons in response to requests, no matter whence they came . . .[7]

Ten days later, Otto Abetz, the German Ambassador in Paris, sent the following supplementary details:

¶ The confidential communication from the German Embassy [at the] Vatican regarding an intervention by the Nuncio in Vichy against the measures adopted against Jews in France are [sic] not entirely without foundation. A few weeks ago, Valerio Valeri broached this matter in conversation with Laval, without mentioning instructions from Rome. Laval did not pursue the matter. Yesterday, Laval stated that at the end of last week the Archbishop of Toulouse issued directions to the priests in his diocese to protest from their pulpits in the sharpest terms against the deportation of the Jews. When this came to Laval's knowledge, he at once summoned Monsignore Rocco, the representative of the absent Nuncio, and pressed him vigorously to notify the Pope and Cardinal Maglione, the Secretary of State, that the French Government would not tolerate such interference in the affairs of the French State. In particular, Laval served notice on Rocco that if the clergy should lend their hands to concealing in churches and monasteries the Jews affected by the deportation order, he would have no compunction in using police to bring them out. Anyway [he said], the anti-Jewish measures were nothing new for the Church because the Popes had been the first to introduce the yellow hat as a means of identifying Jews. The message from the Archbishop of Toulouse

[7] Telegram from Bergen to Berlin, Aug. 18, 1942, StS: V, AA, Bonn (MS).

was read in only some of the churches last Sunday. According to Laval, about half the priests did not obey the instruction, but drew the attention of their prefectures to the subversive intentions of the Archbishop.[8]

Finally, on September 14, Bergen informed Berlin of the latest details he had learned on this matter:

¶ The following confidential information comes to me from sources close to the Vatican: The measures adopted in France against the Jews have strongly aroused the Catholic and clerical elements in that country.

When the Pétain Government took its first steps against the Jews after the armistice, it earned unanimous approval. Those involved in deportation at that time were refugees who had entered from Poland, Romania and other countries and who had been admitted indiscriminately, to the very great detriment of France.

Now, on the other hand, it is the French Jews themselves who are being deported from both the Occupied and Unoccupied Zones and handed over to Germany. This measure has incurred the disapproval of the ecclesiastical authorities, mainly on account of the manner in which it has been carried out. The Archbishops of Paris and Lyons and various other bishops have protested. Within the limits of the possible, the protests have been brought to the notice of the public; they contained no references of any kind to the Vatican.

The French Government has ordered the arrest of those priests who try, by granting lodging or by other measures, to withhold Jews from the deportation order issued against

[8] Telegram from Abetz to Berlin, Aug. 28, 1942, StS: V, AA, Bonn (MS).

them. Thus, a number of priests in the diocese of Lyons have already been arrested, partly because they circulated the protest made by their Archbishops and partly because they refused to hand over children of Jewish race who had been entrusted to them for asylum and shelter.

The démarche made to the French Government by the Vatican to achieve mitigation of the measures against the Jews has so far been without result. The information reaching the Vatican has made a deep impression, and the impression remains.[9]

Among the arrested French priests was the Reverend Father Chaillet, Father Provincial of the Jesuits of Lyons, who was accused of having concealed ninety-two Jewish children.[1]

Part of the French Episcopate and clergy had taken a courageous stand in opposition to the persecution of the Jews.

As early as December 1941, Msgr. Théas, Bishop of Montauban, sent the following letter to the rabbi in his town:

¶ . . . The harassment, the brutal persecution to which your coreligionists are being subjected arouse the protests of the Christian conscience and of all that is honest in the human race.

I am anxious to assure you that you have my very keen sympathy and my prayers. The hour of divine justice will strike. Let us have faith . . .[2]

On June 14, 1942, Father Dillard, in the midst of a service in the Church of Saint-Louis de Vichy, invited his congregation to pray for the prisoners of war, "but also for the 80,000 Frenchmen who are being held up to mockery

9 Telegram from Bergen to Berlin, Sept. 14, 1942, ibid. (MS).
1 Hilberg, op. cit., p. 409.
2 Quoted by Léon Poliakov, op. cit., p. 417.

by being made to wear a yellow star." Father Dillard met his death at Dachau.[3]

On August 30, Msgr. Jules-Gérard Saliège, Archbishop of Toulouse, caused to be read in all the churches of his diocese the pastoral letter mentioned by Abetz in his telegram:

¶ My very dear Brethren,

There is a Christian morality, there is a human morality which imposes duties and recognizes rights. Those duties and those rights are derived from human nature.

They come from God. They can be violated. It does not lie within the power of any mortal to suppress them. It has been reserved to our time to witness the sad spectacle of children, of women, of fathers and mothers being treated like a herd of beasts; to see members of the same family separated one from another and shipped away to an unknown destination. Why is there no longer any right of asylum in our churches? Why are we a conquered people? Lord, have pity on us. Our Lady, pray for France. In our diocese, scenes of horror have taken place in the camps at Noé and Récébédou. Jews are men. Jewesses are women. Foreigners are men, foreign women are women. They cannot be maltreated at will, these men, these women, these fathers and mothers of families. They are part of the human race. They are our brethren as much as are so many others. A Christian cannot forget that. France, our beloved Fatherland; France, which carries in the conscience of all its children the tradition of respect for the human person; chivalrous and generous France, I have no doubt that you are not responsible for these horrors.

---

[3] Nobécourt, op. cit., p. 212.

Yours, in affectionate devotion, Jules-Gérard Saliège. Archbishop of Toulouse.[4]

That same day Msgr. Théas had the following letter read:

¶ I voice the indignant protest of the Christian conscience and I proclaim that all men, Aryan or non-Aryan, are brothers, because they were created by God; that all men, whatever their race or religion, have a right to the respect of individuals and states. The present anti-Semitic measures are a mockery of human dignity, a violation of the most sacred rights of the person and the family.[5]

At that time, public protests were placed on record by several clergymen in the Occupied Zone, such as the parish priests of Saint-Lambert and Saint-Étienne-du-Mont in Paris. Here, by way of example, is the brief sermon delivered in August 1942 by another Paris priest, the *curé* of the parish of Saint-Pierre-du-Gros-Caillou:

¶ You ask me, what is the attitude of Catholics? Know, then, that we are performing the impossible to achieve alleviation of what was originally planned.

My sermon will be short. I know that it may take me to a concentration camp. But it is my duty to repeat that Pius XI condemned racism. So be it.[6]

Yet, at the same time, the Bishops of Nice, of Fréjus and Monaco, as well as the Abbots of Leyrins and Frigolet, sent a telegram reaffirming their loyalty to the Marshal and stating that they dissociated themselves from unpatriotic

4 Quoted by Poliakov, op. cit., p. 418.
5 Quoted by Nobécourt, op. cit., p. 213.
6 Zionist Archives, Jerusalem (MS).

Christians whose apparent concern for the Jews masked a lack of devotion to the regime.[7]

4. Allied Approaches to the Holy See

ON AUGUST 8, 1942, Gerhardt Riegner, the representative of the World Jewish Congress at Geneva, sent the following message to New York through the United States Embassy in Berne:

¶ Received alarming report stating that in Führer's headquarters a plan has been discussed and being under consideration according which total of Jews in countries occupied controlled by Germany numbering three and half to four millions should after deportation and concentration in East be at one blow exterminated in order resolve once for all Jewish Question in Europe. Action is Reported to be planned for autumn ways of execution still discussed. It has been spoken of prussic acid. In transmitting information with all necessary reservation as exactitude cannot be controlled by us beg to state that informer is reported have close connections with highest German authorities and his reports to be generally reliable.[8]

This was the first report concerning "the final solution" as such. Other information, reporting extermination measures in progress in Poland and Russia, had been reaching the Allied capitals since the early summer of 1942. It was at this point that the representatives of the democracies tried to induce the Vatican to take a public stand.

On August 3, 1942, Harold H. Tittmann, the American

---

[7] Eugen Weber: *L'Action française* (Paris: Stock; 1964), p. 507.
[8] Archives of the World Jewish Congress, Geneva (MS).

representative at the Holy See in the absence of Myron C.
Taylor, sent the following telegram to the State Department:

¶ In recent reports to the Department, I have called attention to the opinion that the failure of the Holy See to protest publicly against Nazi atrocities is endangering its moral
prestige and is undermining faith both in the Church and
in the Holy Father himself. I have on a number of occasions
informally reminded the Vatican of this danger and so have
certain of my colleagues but without result. The answer is
invariably that the Pope in his speeches has already condemned offenses against morality in wartime and that to
be specific now would only make matters worse.

Yesterday the Brazilian Ambassador to the Holy See
called on me to inquire whether I would be prepared to
join in a concerted (not collective but rather simultaneous)
démarche to persuade the Pope to condemn publicly and
in specific terms the Nazi atrocities in German-occupied
areas. Monsieur Accioly said that he had already received
the necessary instructions from his Government for him to
take part in such a *démarche* and was endeavoring to enlist
the co-operation of the representatives of Great Britain,
Poland, Belgium, Yugoslavia and as many Latin American
countries as possible. The Belgian Ambassador has already
agreed and the British Minister and Polish Ambassador are
telegraphing for instructions. The Polish Ambassador tells
me furthermore that he is under the impression that his
Government may have recently made soundings in the
above sense among certain Allied Governments.

While I doubt very much that the Pope can be moved
to take the desired action I cannot see that the *démarche*
could do any harm and I believe it would serve to reinforce

the individual reminders that have heretofore been made.

If the Department feels that it is desirable that I take part in such a *démarche* I would appreciate receiving instructions at an early date.[9]

On August 4, Secretary of State Cordell Hull replied:

¶ In the event the Brazilian Ambassador endeavors to have the Pope publicly condemn the Nazi atrocities in German-occupied areas, and you are informed of such action, you are authorized to make an independent but simultaneous approach to the Vatican Foreign Office and to point out the universal condemnation of these cruel and inhuman actions by the Hitler forces and the universal condemnation which has been reflected in the expressions of all free peoples at these incredible horrors. You may also point out the helpful effect of a similar condemnation on the part of the Pope in bringing about some check on the unbridled and uncalled for actions of the Nazi forces.[1]

Some days later, the American Undersecretary of State, Sumner Welles, described a conversation he had just had with the British Minister in Washington:

¶ Sir Ronald Campbell called to see me this morning at his request. The Minister stated that the British Minister at the Vatican had been authorized to make simultaneous approaches to the Cardinal Secretary of State with other representatives of the United Nations, upon the initiative of the Brazilian Ambassador, to urge that the Vatican do what

[9] Telegram from Tittmann to Washington of Aug. 3, 1942, *Foreign Relations of the United States* (hereinafter called *FRUS*), III, pp. 772–3.
[1] Telegram from Hull to Tittmann, Aug. 4, 1942, ibid., p. 773.

might be possible publicly to condemn the assassination
and abuse by Germany of innocent persons in occupied
territories. I told the Minister that the American representative, Mr. Tittmann, had already been authorized to the
same effect.[2]

Thereupon, on September 14, Tittmann sent the following note to Cardinal Maglione:

¶ In accordance with instructions received from his Government, the Chargé d'Affaires of the United States to the Holy
See has the honor to call the attention of His Eminence
the Cardinal Secretary of State to the cruel and inhuman
treatment by the Hitler forces of the civil populations in
areas occupied by the Germans. He desires to point out
that these incredible horrors have been universally condemned and that this universal condemnation has been
reflected in the expressions of all free peoples.

The Chargé d'Affaires has also been authorized by his
Government to point out the helpful effect that a similar
condemnation of these atrocities by the Holy Father would
have in bringing about some check on the unbridled and
uncalled-for actions of the forces of the Nazi regime.[3]

Brazil, Great Britain, Belgium, Poland, Uruguay and
Yugoslavia sent notes in much the same terms to the Secretariat of State. A few days later, Myron C. Taylor delivered
to Cardinal Maglione a note that was infinitely more explicit:

[2] Memorandum by Sumner Welles, Aug. 18, 1942, ibid., p. 773.
[3] Memorandum from Tittmann to Maglione, Sept. 14, 1942, ibid.,
p. 774.

¶ Vatican City, September 26, 1942.

My Dear Cardinal Maglione: I have the honor to bring to the attention of Your Eminence the following memorandum which has been received from my Government:

"The following was received from the Geneva Office of the Jewish Agency for Palestine in a letter dated August 30th, 1942. That office received the report from two reliable eyewitnesses (Aryans), one of whom came on August 14th from Poland.

"1) Liquidation of the Warsaw Ghetto is taking place. Without any distinction all Jews, irrespective of age or sex, are being removed from the Ghetto in groups and shot. Their corpses are utilized for making fats and their bones for the manufacture of fertilizer. Corpses are even being exhumed for these purposes.

"2) These mass executions take place, not in Warsaw, but in especially prepared camps for the purpose, one of which is stated to be in Belzek. About 50,000 Jews have been executed in Lemberg itself on the spot during the past month. According to another report, 100,000 have been massacred in Warsaw. There is not one Jew left in the entire district east of Poland, including occupied Russia. It is also reported, in this connection, that the entire non-Jewish population of Sebastopol was murdered. So as not to attract the attention of foreign countries, the butchering of the Jewish population in Poland was not done at one single time.

"3) Jews deported from Germany, Belgium, Holland, France, and Slovakia are sent to be butchered, while Aryans deported to the East from Holland and France are genuinely used for work.

"4) Inasmuch as butcherings of this kind would attract great attention in the west [sic], they must first of all deport them to the East, where less opportunity is afforded to outsiders of knowing what is going on. During the last few weeks a large part of the Jewish population deported to Lithuania and Lublin has already been executed. That is probably the reason why the deportees were not permitted to have correspondence with any one. A great number of the German refugees were taken to Theresienstadt. This place, however, is only an interim station and the people there await the same fate.

"5) Arrangements are made for new deportations as soon as space is made by executions. Caravans of such deportees being transported in cattle cars are often seen. There are about forty people in each cattle car . . ."

I should much appreciate it if Your Eminence could inform me whether the Vatican has any information that would tend to confirm the reports contained in this memorandum. If so, I should like to know whether the Holy Father has any suggestions as to any practical manner in which the forces of civilized public opinion could be utilized in order to prevent a continuation of these barbarities.[4]

On October 6, Tittmann informed the State Department that other Latin-American countries had associated themselves with the initiative of the Brazilian Ambassador, M. Accioly. The Chargé d'Affaires added:

¶ It would appear that M. Accioly's efforts are having the full and active support of the Jesuits. . . .

I understand that the Pope is giving careful considera-

---

[4] Letter from Myron C. Taylor to Cardinal Maglione, Sept. 26, 1942, ibid., pp. 775 f.

tion to the matter and the general impression is that he will say something at an opportune moment. Opinion in the Vatican seems to be divided as to the wisdom of the Accioly *démarche*. . . .

The Holy See is still apparently convinced that a forthright denunciation by the Pope of Nazi atrocities, at least in so far as Poland is concerned, would only result in the violent deaths of many more people. Msgr. Montini, however, stated to me that the time may come when, in spite of such a grievous prospect, the Holy Father will feel himself obliged to speak out.

. . . Another motive, possibly the controlling one, behind the Pope's disinclination to denounce Nazi atrocities is his fear that if he does so now, the German people, in the bitterness of their defeat, will reproach him later on for having contributed, if only indirectly, to this defeat. It has been pointed out to me that just such an accusation was directed against the Holy See by the Germans after the last war, because of certain phrases spoken . . . by Benedict XV while hostilities were in progress. When it is borne in mind that Pius XII had many years of conditioning in Germany, it will not seem unnatural that he should be particularly sensible to this particular argument.[5]

On October 10, 1942, Tittmann transmitted the answer sent by the Secretariat of State:

¶ Holy See replied today to Mr. Taylor's letter regarding the predicament of the Jews in Poland in an informal and unsigned statement handed me by the Cardinal Secretary of State [wrote Tittman].

After thanking Ambassador Taylor for bringing the

[5] Telegram from Tittmann to Washington, Oct. 6, 1942, ibid., pp. 776 f.

matter to the attention of the Holy See the statement says that reports of severe measures taken against non-Aryans have also reached the Holy See from other sources but that up to the present time it has not been possible to verify the accuracy thereof. However, the statement adds it is well known that the Holy See is taking advantage of every opportunity offered in order to mitigate the suffering of non-Aryans.

I regret [Tittmann concluded] that Holy See could not have been more helpful but it was evident from the attitude of the Cardinal that it has no practical suggestions to make. I think it is perhaps likely that the belief is held that there is little hope of checking Nazi barbarities by any method except that of physical force coming from without.[6]

On December 17, all the Allied nations officially condemned the extermination of the Jews by the Nazis and served notice that those responsible would not escape punishment:

¶ The above-mentioned governments and the French National Committee condemn in the strongest possible terms this bestial policy of cold-blooded extermination. They declare that such events can only strengthen the resolve of all freedom-loving peoples to overthrow the barbarous Hitlerite tyranny. They reaffirm their solemn resolution to insure that those responsible for these crimes shall not escape retribution and to press on with the necessary practical measures to this end.[7]

The American Government then made one more attempt to induce the Holy See to take an open stand. On Christmas Eve, Tittmann sent Hull the following telegram:

[6] Telegram from Tittmann to Hull, Oct. 10, 1942, ibid., pp. 777 f.
[7] *U. S. State Department Bulletin,* 1942, p. 1009.

¶ In a recent conversation with the Cardinal Secretary of State I referred to the Joint Declaration of the United Nations on the mass extermination of the Jews in German occupied countries and asked him whether there was not something Holy See could do along similar lines. He replied as before to the effect that Holy See was unable to denounce publicly particular atrocities but that it had frequently condemned atrocities in general. He added that everything possible was being done privately to relieve the distress of the Jews. Although deploring cruelties that have come to his attention he said that Holy See was unable to verify Allied reports as to the number of Jews exterminated *et cetera.*

There are rumors to the effect that the Pope in his Christmas message will take a strong stand on this subject but I am afraid that any deviation from the generalities of his previous messages is unlikely.[8]

At the end of 1942, the Holy See had obtained a report that was perhaps even more precise than that of the Jewish organizations or of the Allies: the report of S.S. Colonel Kurt Gerstein.

5. *The Gerstein Report*

ROLF HOCHHUTH'S PLAY, *The Deputy,* made famous the figure of Colonel Kurt Gerstein, who joined the S.S. to "see" what was happening and publish the facts to the world.

In August 1942, Gerstein, who had just witnessed a mass extermination by gas, tried to obtain an interview with Nuncio Orsenigo; he was turned away. He then handed a re-

---

[8] Telegram from Tittmann to Hull (transmitted by Harrison on Dec. 26, 1942), *FRUS,* 1942, I, pp. 70 f.

port to the legal adviser to Msgr. Preysing, Archbishop of Berlin, with the request that it be forwarded to the Holy See.[9] There is no reason to believe that the text was not sent to Rome.

Gerstein's Report of 1942 was probably almost identical with the report which he drew up on May 4, 1945, since it describes the same event; in 1942, in fact, the Colonel was in a position to recall the details with greater accuracy than would be the case three years later. As for the veracity of Gerstein's statements, no historian seriously casts doubt on them.

It is not inappropriate to reproduce here a brief extract from the 1945 report because, bearing in mind that the Holy See has not denied to this day that it received the Gerstein Report during the war, one is entitled to assume that a text largely similar to that which we are about to quote was forwarded to the Sovereign Pontiff by Msgr. Preysing at the end of 1942.

Gerstein was at the Belsen [Belzek] Camp:

¶ . . . A train arrived from Lemberg [Lvov]. There were forty-five cars containing 6,700 people, 1,450 of whom were already dead. Through the gratings on the windows, children could be seen peering out, terribly pale and frightened, their eyes filled with mortal dread, as well as men and women. The train entered the station, and 200 Ukrainians wrenched open the doors and drove the people out of the carriages with their leather whips. Instructions came through a large loudspeaker, telling them to remove all their clothing, artificial limbs, glasses, etc. They were to hand over all objects of value at the counter, without being given a ticket or receipt. Shoes were to be carefully tied

[9] "Augenzeugenbericht zu den Massenvergasungen," *Vierteljahreshefte für Zeitgeschichte,* I (1953), p. 193.

together (for the collection of textiles), for otherwise no one would ever again have been able to find shoes belonging to each other in a pile that was a good 80 feet high. Then the women and girls were sent to the barber who, with two or three strokes of his scissors, cut off all their hair and dropped it into potato sacks. "That's for some special purpose or other on U-Boats, for packing or something like that," I was told by an S.S.-Unterscharführer who was on duty there.

Then the column moved off. Headed by an extremely pretty young girl, they walked along the avenue, all naked, men, women and children, with artificial limbs removed. I myself was stationed up on the ramp between the [gas] chambers with Captain Wirth.

Mothers with babies at their breasts came up, hesitated, and entered the chambers of death. At the corner stood a burly S.S. man with a priest-like voice. "Nothing at all is going to happen to you!" he told the poor wretches. "All you have to do when you get into the chambers is to breathe in deeply. That stretches the lungs. Inhaling is necessary to prevent disease and epidemics." When asked what would be done with them, he replied: "Well, of course, the men will have to work building houses and roads, but the women won't need to work. They can do housework or help in the kitchen, but only if they want to." For some of these poor creatures, this was a small ray of hope that was enough to make them walk the few steps to the chambers without resistance. Most of them knew what was going on. The smell told them what their fate was to be. They went up the small flight of steps and saw everything. Mothers with their babies clasped to their breasts, small children, adults, men, women, all naked; they hesitated, but they entered the chambers of death, thrust forward by the others behind them or by the leather whips of the S.S. Most went in without a word . . . Many were saying prayers. I prayed with them. I pressed myself into a corner and cried aloud to my God and theirs. How gladly I should have gone into the chambers with them; how gladly I should have died with them. Then they would have found an S.S. officer in uniform in their gas chambers; they would have believed it was an accident and the story would have been buried and forgotten. But I could not do that yet. First, I had to make known what I had seen here. The chambers were filling up. Fill them up well—that was Captain Wirth's order. The people were treading on each other's feet. There were 700-800 of them in an area of 270 square feet, in 1,590 cubic feet of space. The S.S. crushed them together as tightly as they possibly could. The doors closed. Meanwhile, the rest waited out in the open, all naked. "It's done exactly the same way in winter," I was told. "But they may catch their death!" I said. "That's what they're here for," an S.S. man said. . . . The Diesel exhaust gases were intended to kill those unfortunates. But the engine was not working. . . . The people in the gas chambers waited, in vain. I heard them weeping, sobbing. . . . After 2 hours and 49 minutes, measured by my stop watch, the Diesel started. Up to that moment, men and women had been shut up alive in those 4 chambers, 4 times 750 people in 4 times 1590 cubic feet of space. Another 25 minutes dragged by. Many of those inside were already dead. They could be seen through the small window when the electric light went on for a moment and lit up the inside of the chamber. After 28 minutes, few were left alive. At the end of 32 minutes, all were dead.

In his 1945 report, Gerstein added:

¶ I tried . . . to inform the Apostolic Nuncio in Berlin. There, I was asked if I was a soldier. After that, all further discussion with me was refused and I was asked to leave His Holiness's Embassy . . . I then reported all of this to hundreds of persons, among them, Dr. Winter, the syndic to the Catholic Bishop of Berlin, with the request that the information be forwarded to the Pope . . ."

It may be argued that even if the Gerstein Report had reached the Holy See, it would have failed to carry conviction on account of the strange personality of its author. How could anyone believe an S.S. man who claimed to be hostile to the regime to the point of divulging such secrets? Was he not mentally disturbed? In point of fact, such an objection is barely plausible, because all that the Gerstein Report did was to verify and confirm the reports of Jewish organizations, of the Allies and of various German officers, one of whom at least had come specially from the Russian front to inform Cardinal Faulhaber of what he had witnessed.[1]

Lastly, we may note that in a letter of November 8, 1942, Msgr. Sapieha, Archbishop of Cracow, complained to Governor General Frank that Polish workers had been used to take part in the extermination of Jews.[2]

[1] Cf. the contribution by Thomas Dehler in Fritz J. Raddatz, ed.: *Summa injuria, oder durfte der Papst schweigen?* (Reinbek bei Hamburg: Rowohlt; 1963), p. 231.
[2] Letter quoted by Léon Poliakov in "The Vatican and the Jewish Question," *Commentary*, November 1950, p. 442. Note, as did M. Poliakov, the terrible ambiguity of Msgr. Sapieha's phrase.

6. *Pope Pius's Christmas Message, 1942*

HAROLD TITTMANN had written in December 1942 that "there are rumors to the effect that the Pope in his Christmas message will take a strong stand. . . . But I am afraid that any deviation from the generalities of his previous messages is unlikely."

In fact, Pius XII was to say something, and, as shown by the documents presented in the following pages, he seems to have believed that he had been very explicit. It is impossible to reproduce here the complete text of that Christmas message, which was very long. Let us confine ourselves to the twenty-fourth page of the twenty-six it covers, on which the passage in question occurs.

¶ Do the nations, then, wish to remain passive witnesses of the disastrous progress (of the war)? Is it not, rather, incumbent on all righteous and magnanimous hearts to unite on the ruins of a system of public order which has given such tragic proof of its incapacity to assure the well-being of the people? To unite and to take a solemn vow never to rest until, among all the peoples and all the nations of the earth, the names of those shall be legion who are resolved to lead society back to the divine law, the indestructible center of gravity, and whose aspiration is to dedicate themselves to the service of the human person and of the community ennobled in God?

Humanity owes this vow to that infinite, suffering multitude of mothers, widows and orphans who have seen their lives robbed of light, strength, and support. Humanity owes this vow to the countless exiles whom the hurricane of war has torn from their native homes, scattering them in foreign lands, and who could make the prophet's lament their own.

Humanity owes this vow to hundreds of thousands of people who, through no fault of their own and solely because of their nation or their race, have been condemned to death or progressive extinction. [Author's italics.]

Humanity owes this vow to the thousands upon thousands of noncombatants—women, children, the sick and the aged; those whom the air war—and we have, from the outset, often denounced its horrors—has deprived, without distinction, of life, possessions, health, homes, refuges, and places of worship.

The reference to those who, by the mere fact of their nation or race, were doomed to die or suffer progressive extinction seems to have escaped the notice of most of the Pope's listeners and, above all, of the Germans; none of the Wilhelmstrasse documents devoted to an analysis of the Pontiff's message dwells on this point.

The Poles were the first to protest, indirectly, against the extreme reserve of the Pope's message. On January 2, 1943, less than ten days after the Christmas message, Wladislaw Raczkiewicz, President of the Polish Government in exile, addressed a particularly moving letter to the Holy Father. "The obvious proof," writes Carlo Falconi, "that the Polish President regarded the papal message as most ill-suited to such a dramatic situation is that he did not even speak of it in his letter." The importance of this appeal far exceeds its literary and emotional value; it stems above all from the courageous passages in which he said that the Polish people were less in need of material or diplomatic help than of an unequivocal and unquestionable denunciation of the evil and of those responsible for it; it derives, perhaps, even more from the passages which proclaimed that what the Poles needed was to be confirmed in the certainty that "divine law knows no compromise." The text of the letter is as follows:

¶ Holy Father:

Divine laws trampled underfoot; human dignity degraded; hundreds of thousands of men murdered without judgment; families separated; churches profaned and closed; religion in the catacombs: such is the picture of Poland that emerges from the reports we receive from our country.

At this tragic moment, my people are fighting not merely for their lives but for everything that has been sacred in their eyes. They want justice, not vengeance. They do not ask so much for material or diplomatic help, because they know that the possibilities of their receiving such help are slim, *but they implore that a voice be raised to show clearly and plainly where the evil lies and to condemn those in the service of evil.* [Author's italics.]

If these people can be reinforced in their conviction that divine law knows no compromise and that it stands above any human considerations of the moment, they will, I am sure, find the strength to resist. This stiffening will enable them to preserve the spirit of superhuman courage which led the Catholics of Warsaw to protest, in the name of Christian principles, against the violence done to the Jews and against their murder, even though each word of their appeal might have brought down upon them the most dire suppression.

At certain times of trial in Poland's past, moments which were less fraught with tears and blood than is now the case, Your Holiness's great predecessors addressed fatherly words to the Polish people. Today, when throughout the bulk of our territory it is no longer possible to preach or pray in the Polish tongue, the Apostolic See must break silence so that those who die, without benefit of religion, in defense of their faith and their traditions may receive the blessing of the successor of Christ.

Such is the prayer of my suffering nation, which, conscious of my responsibilities as Chief of State, I lay at the feet of Your Holiness.

Wladislaw Raczkiewicz

London, January 2, 1943.[3]

Shortly after Christmas, Harold Tittmann had an interview with the Pope:

¶ With regard to his Christmas message, [wrote Tittmann] the Pope gave me the impression that he was sincere in believing that he had spoken therein clearly enough to satisfy all those who had been insisting in the past that he utter some word of condemnation of the Nazi atrocities, and he seemed surprised when I told him that I thought there were some who did not share his belief.

He said that he thought that it was plain to everyone that he was referring to the Poles, Jews, and hostages when he declared that hundreds of thousands of persons had been killed or tortured through no fault of their own, sometimes only because of their race or nationality.

He explained that when talking of atrocities he could not name the Nazis without at the same time mentioning the Bolsheviks and this he thought might not be wholly pleasing to the Allies. He stated that he "feared" that there was foundation for the atrocity reports of the Allies but led me to believe that he felt that there had been some exaggera-

---

[3] Quoted in Carlo Falconi, op. cit., pp. 282 f.

tion for purposes of propaganda. Taken as a whole he thought his message should be welcomed by the American people and I agreed with (him).[4]

In the circumstances, the Pope's remarks are particularly difficult to interpret. The phrase "some exaggeration for purposes of propaganda" is not very clear if the numerous unanimous reports which probably had reached the Holy See in 1942 are taken into account. As to the Bolshevik atrocities mentioned by the Sovereign Pontiff, what was he referring to? In the period from 1939 to 1944, the event that comes to mind is the massacre of the 11,000 Polish officers stationed at Katyn, which by general agreement is attributed to the Russians. But the first news concerning that massacre was disseminated by the Germans—the parties most interested in getting it published—in April 1943, that is, several months after the interview between Tittmann and the Pope. Consequently, the Pope was probably not referring to anything definite and was simply condemning the Bolsheviks in general terms.

We have touched here, *en passant,* on something which seemingly was to become the major preoccupation of the Holy See from 1943 onward: the Bolshevik threat. By referring to Bolshevik atrocities, which in January 1943 were probably difficult to specify more closely, and by invoking that argument to explain his silence in the face of the massacre of Jews, the Sovereign Pontiff could give the impression that there was a link between that silence and his fear of the Bolshevik threat. In effect, to condemn the Germans would weaken the Reich as the rampart against Bolshevism. Obviously, this is no more than a hypothesis which no text explicitly proves.

[4] Telegram from Tittmann to Hull, Jan. 5, 1943, *FRUS,* 1943, II, p. 912.
[5] Cf. Chapter VII.

It should be noted, lastly, that we already have at our disposal two different explanations given by the Holy See to justify its silence: that of Cardinal Maglione, who indicated that the Pope could not denounce specific atrocities; and that of Pius XII, who stressed that he could only denounce German atrocities if he denounced Bolshevik atrocities at the same time. The Pope was to give other explanations in his letter to Msgr. Preysing in April 1943 and in his address to the Sacred College of Cardinals in June of the same year.

7. *The Pope's Letter to Msgr. Preysing and Address to the Sacred College of Cardinals*

ON APRIL 30, 1943, Pius XII sent the following letter to Msgr. Preysing, Archbishop of Berlin:

¶ We should like first of all, venerable Brother, to thank you for the good wishes which you have sent Us, personally and in the name of your clergy and of your diocese, on various occasions, notably in December for festivals at the turn of the year and on the anniversary of our election to the Sovereign Pontificate. We know how loyal and full of the spirit of faith is the heart from which they come. We thank you particularly, you and your flock, for your holy prayers. In your letter of February 27 last, you assure Us of your fervent prayers, in full consciousness that "rarely has God imposed such a heavy burden on the shoulders of a Pope at the beginning of his pontificate, with this frightful World War and all the evils and sins which are its consequences." Certainly, one must always show prudence in comparing the present with the past. We do not wish to underestimate in any way the preoccupations and tribulations that weighed upon the shoulders of Our predecessors. However, the Pope's sincere wish to go to meet, in full impartiality, all the powers of the world as they face each other in the vast turmoil of this conflict—and at the same time to protect the Holy Church solicitously against its consequences—has rarely confronted the Holy See with such heavy trials as at this time. But the greatest preoccupation is, as you so rightly say, "the evils and sins which are the consequence of the war." The cruelty of the technique of war, which is developing with unbridled violence, makes it impossible to bear the prospect that this mutual massacre may yet continue for a long time. Day after day, knowledge reaches Us of inhuman acts which have nothing whatever to do with the real necessities of war and which fill us with consternation and terror. Prayer alone, prayer to the God who sees all, in the tabernacle of the Redeemer, enables us to find the moral strength to overcome in Our mind the impression caused by such acts.

The Nazi Attitude to the Pope's Efforts to Soften the Inhumanity of the War

You, too, must have known the terrible experience of war in the painful form of bombing from the air. We say, once again, to you and to the members of your diocese how much We deplore, with you, the destruction of St. Hedwig's Cathedral as a result of the last raid on Berlin. Your congregation should know that We offer a special prayer and a special benediction every day for those who on that day, in one camp or another, fall victim to aerial bombardment. We are doing what lies in Our power to mitigate the evils of the war, and We work unceasingly, undeterred by the meagre prospects of success, with the object of ensuring that the civil population is spared as far as possible. It is not Our fault if complete fairness in the face of the problems posed by the war obliges Us—now that it is Germany that is suffering most heavily from air attack—to mediate discreetly; We do so regardless of the fact that the German authorities, in consequence of the presence in Rome of the Archbishop of New York, or, rather, because of the rumors circulating on the subject of his visit to Rome, have let it be known publicly that Germany is not interested in the Pope's efforts to humanize the war. In Our efforts to that end, We are moved by equal solicitude for all the war's victims, for all those who, because of it, are suffering materially or morally. In Germany, as in the rest of the world, those people are placing their hopes in Our help.

It would have been Our dearest wish to have Our news service for prisoners of war operate for the benefit of Germany as much as other countries. It was as a result of requests for intervention made to the Holy See—requests to which, in many instances, other authorities would have been unable to respond—that this service developed spontaneously to its present state. Simultaneously with Our other war work—and for this We give thanks to God—it has been able to do much good. We fail to understand what motive can have induced the German authorities to deny access to German territory for Pontifical activities. This prohibition was particularly keenly felt here when it involved some thousand or so items of information concerning German prisoners which had been addressed to Our service for transmission to their families in Germany. We finally achieved this, but by devious means and with the greatest difficulty. Since the autumn of 1942, ever growing numbers of inquiries have been coming in from Germany about men who have disappeared or been taken prisoner on the Russian front, chiefly at Stalingrad. These approaches offer evidence of overpowering distress. We, for our part, will take all possible steps to secure information about prisoners in Russia, but, unhappily, we have so far obtained absolutely no result.

The Pastoral Letters of the German Bishops

We are grateful to you, Venerable Brother, for the clear and frank words which, in various circumstances, you have addressed to your congregation and, through them, to the public. We have in mind, among others, your statements of June 28, 1942, on the Christian conception of law; that of All Souls' Sunday last, on the right of every man to life and love; We think especially of your Advent pastoral letter, which was also adopted in the ecclesiastical provinces of Western Germany, on the sovereign rights of God, the rights of the individual and the rights of the family.

Let no man claim that courageous stands by Bishops injure your country in world opinion when they demand from their government the rights of religion, of the Church, and of the human person, on behalf of those who are defenseless and who are oppressed by public authority, whether the victims are children of the Church or not. Far from compromising your country, this courageous defense of right and humanity will earn both it and you the respect of world opinion and it may yield benefits in the future.

As Supreme Pastor of the flock, We are concerned that the conviction and faith of your Catholics shall remain unmarred by compromise with principles and acts that are contrary to the law of God and the spirit of Christ and

[138]

which often even hold them up to ridicule. To take a recent example, it was a consolation for Us to learn that Catholics, notably in Berlin, had manifested great Christian charity toward the sufferings of "non-Aryans." Let this be the occasion for Us to express Our paternal gratitude and Our profound sympathy to Msgr. Lichtenberg who is in prison.

But it pains us even to think that, progressively, perhaps almost unconsciously, by dint of habit and incessant propaganda, these concepts may penetrate the minds of Catholics. You know that liturgical questions which have arisen in your diocese have been considered sufficiently important to command the attention of the Holy See. Nonetheless, We acknowledge that We attach infinitely more importance to protecting the conscience of Christians against all the poisons threatening that conscience. What would be the use of embellishing the liturgy of the Church if, outside the Church, the thought and acts of Catholics in their lives were to become alien to the law and the love of Christ?

Reasons for the Pope's Reserve

So far as episcopal declarations are concerned, We leave to pastors on the spot the task of assessing whether, and to what extent, the danger of reprisals and pressures and, perhaps, other circumstances due to the length and the psychological climate of the war, counsel restraint—despite reasons that might exist for intervention—in order to avoid greater evils. This is one of the motives for the limitations which We impose on Ourself in Our declarations. The experience We gained in 1942, when We allowed papal documents to be freely reproduced for the use of Catholics, justifies Our attitude, so far as we can see.

[139]

We have spoken at length on these questions, not because you need Our exhortation to act, but because, on the one hand, We know your courage and your great concern for the honor of the Holy Church and, on the other, because We know that you judge the situation cautiously and coolly. For the representative of Christ, the path he must travel to keep a just balance between the contradictory demands of his pastoral responsibility is becoming ever harder and stonier.

The measures against the Church, of which you informed Us in your letter, are in Our thoughts: confiscation of ecclesiastical property; seizure of your seminary at Hedwigshöhe; restrictions on, or prohibition of, the apostolate to the Poles deported to Germany, or of religious instruction to Polish children; prohibition of marriage for Poles, etc. All of this has been, and is, only part of a vast plan which aims at stifling the life of the Church in the territory where the German writ runs. Most severely affected, as you know, is the Catholic Church in the Warthegau. The unspeakable distress of the faithful in that region causes us acute suffering, the more so as all attempts to intervene with the Government on their behalf have been brutally rebuffed. The considerations of which we spoke earlier—and, in the special case of the Warthegau, the fear, above all, that what is left there in the way of pastoral life may be threatened in its turn—have restrained Us up to now from openly denouncing the situation under which the Church is laboring there.

We are relatively well informed on the situation and the fate of priests in concentration camps, among whom the Polish priests form by far the largest number. If any possibility of doing so occurs, all the priests and their companions in captivity should be told that they are the object of Our profound sympathy; that at this time of suffering and cruelty there are few whose fate is as close to Our heart as theirs; and that We pray for them earnestly every day.

We have before us the text of the memorandum addressed by the German Episcopate to the Government of the Reich. You can now see for yourself how little chance of success a confidential petition addressed to the government can have. However, come what may, that memorandum will serve after the war to justify the Episcopate in the eyes of the world.

Action of the Holy See on Behalf of the Jews

To non-Aryan Catholics as well as those of the Jewish faith, the Holy See has acted charitably, within the limits of its responsibilities, on the material and moral plane. This action has necessitated a great deal of patience and disinterestedness on the part of the executive arms of Our relief organizations in meeting the expectations—one might even say demands—of those asking for help, and also in overcoming the diplomatic difficulties that have arisen. Let us not speak of the very large sums in American money which We have had to disburse on shipping for emigrants. We gave those sums willingly because the people concerned were in distress. The money was given for the love of God, and We were right not to expect gratitude on this earth. Nevertheless, Jewish organizations have warmly thanked the Holy See for these rescue operations.

In Our Christmas message We said a word about the things that are presently being done to non-Aryans in the territories under German authority. It was short, but it was well understood. It is superfluous to say that Our paternal love and solicitude are greater today toward non-Aryan or semi-Aryan Catholics, children of the Church like the others, when their outward existence is collapsing and they are going through moral distress. Unhappily, in the present circumstances, We cannot offer them effective help other than through Our prayers. We are, however, determined to raise Our voice anew on their behalf as circumstances indicate and permit.

Nazi Education

We have heard very consoling things these past few days concerning the unswerving fidelity of German Catholics to their faith and their Church. Above and beyond all matters for disquiet and despair, there remains for Us a single grave question regarding the future. Catholic youth has been subjected completely to the influence and the education of a closed system, a system alien to Christianity and built upon the organization of the Party and the precepts, already known, of the future *Volksgesetzbuch* [People's Law Code]. How will that rising generation be able to keep intact, and hand on, its Catholic faith? We find consolation only in this promise of the Scripture: "God is faithful, who will not suffer you to be tempted above that which you are able: but will make also with temptation issue, that you may be able to bear it" (I Cor. 10, 13).

As a pledge of those words, "will make also with temptation issue," We bestow upon you "under the sign of the cross," as you put it in your pastoral letter for the last "Sunday of the Pope"—upon you, Venerable Brother, upon your collaborators in the Apostolate and on all the members of your diocese, the solicited Apostolic blessing. We do so with paternal affection and with all Our heart.[6]

Lastly, on June 2, 1943, Pius XII raised the problem of the extermination of the Jews in a secret address to the Sacred College of Cardinals, and explained yet again his extreme restraint.

Calling attention to "the anxious entreaties of all those who, because of their nationality or their race, are being subjected to overwhelming trials and sometimes, through no fault of their own, are doomed to extermination," he added:

¶ Every word We address to the competent authority on this subject, and all Our public utterances, have to be carefully weighed and measured by Us in the interests of the victims themselves, lest, contrary to Our intentions, We make their situation worse and harder to bear. To put the matter at its lowest, the ameliorations apparently obtained do not match the scope of the Church's maternal solicitude on behalf of the particular groups that are suffering the most appalling fate. The Vicar of Christ, who asked no more than pity and a sincere return to elementary standards of justice and humanity, then found himself facing a door that no key could open.[7]

It is notable that, in his letter to Msgr. Preysing, the Sovereign Pontiff referred to the material aid given to the Jews by the Holy See during the first years of the war. The information available on this point is contradictory and does not enable us to assess the extent of this aid. The figures and details

---

[6] The text of this letter was published in the *Documentation Catholique,* Paris, Feb. 2, 1964.
[7] The text of the address was published in Alexis Curvers: *Pie XII, Le Pape outragé* (Paris: Laffont; 1964), p. 139.

vary considerably according to the authors concerned, and the latter—whether it be Robert P. Leiber, Guenter Lewy or others—themselves do not supply precise references to documentary sources. But the essence of the letter from Pius XII to Msgr. Preysing does not lie there. What should capture all the reader's attention is the explanation given by the Sovereign Pontiff of the reasons for his own restraint and of the fact that the Bishops were left free to judge for themselves.

It is not appropriate for us, in the context of this study, to attempt to judge whether the reasons adduced by the Sovereign Pontiff to explain the liberty of action given to the Bishops, as well as his own restraint, seem, *after the event,* valid or not. Contrariwise, comment on specific matters of detail may help in facilitating an assessment. Thus, as regards the liberty of action given to the Bishops, the Orthodox Church, at that time, seems to have adopted a different attitude. According to information supplied to the Chief Rabbi of Palestine, the Orthodox Patriarch of Constantinople sent a note to all his Bishops in the Balkans and in Central Europe, enjoining them to help the Jews with all the means in their power and to proclaim in the churches that concealing Jews was a sacred duty.[8]

This might possibly explain the paradoxical fact that in Slovakia, an essentially Catholic country, more Jews were able to escape deportation, for the moment, by "conversion" to the Orthodox religion than by "conversion" to Catholicism.[9] The difference in attitude on the part of the Bishops seems, in this matter, to have played an important role.

[8] Zalman Shragai: *Chief Rabbi Herzog's Rescue Mission* (in Hebrew). Jerusalem, 1947, p. 6.
[9] Hilberg: op. cit., p. 466.

So far as the Pope's reasons for his own restraint are concerned, they are recapitulated in his address to the Sacred College. Now this latter text gives the impression that the Sovereign Pontiff, before resigning himself to silence, had approached the Germans, but without the slightest result: "The Vicar of Christ . . . then found himself facing a door that no key could open."[1] However, apart from three interventions by Nuncio Orsenigo which we shall mention later, the Wilhelmstrasse Archives do not contain any document recording a discussion of the Jewish problem between the Pope and one of the Reich Ambassadors or between the Secretary of State and the German diplomats. The possibility remains that Msgr. Orsenigo may have made a direct approach to Hitler and that the minutes of the interview have disappeared with most of the files of the Reich Chancellery. If such an interview did take place, it may be hoped that the Vatican Archives will reveal its contents to us soon.

8. Msgr. Orsenigo's Interventions

ON OCTOBER 15, 1942, Woermann wrote:

¶ Today, the Nuncio, somewhat embarrassed and without pressing the point, brought up the fact that a number of inquiries had come to the Vatican from Jews, asking about the fate of relatives who had been made to leave their previous places of residence. Such inquiries (he said) concerned Jews from France and Lemberg [Lvov].

I told the Nuncio I could not give him any information on this question.

[1] For another possible explanation of this phrase, see p. 167.

The Nuncio said that in that case he would report to Rome that he had raised the matter here but had been unable to obtain any information.[2]

The second intervention took place some weeks later.

On November 6, Weizsäcker wrote a note on the following conversation with Msgr. Orsenigo:

¶ As the Nuncio was leaving today, he casually mentioned rumors of an impending intensification of the ordinances concerning mixed marriages. The Nuncio claimed to have heard that in future such mixed marriages would have to be dissolved. Without entering into the dogmatic doctrine of the Catholic Church, he wished to urge me to keep an eye on this impending legislation.

I did not get involved in any factual discussion of the subject.[3]

The last intervention by Msgr. Orsenigo took place in August 1943. The Apostolic Nuncio handed State Secretary Steengracht (who had replaced Weizsäcker) a *note verbale* regarding a certain Fanny Adler, a seventy-four-year-old Jewess who found herself completely destitute in Amsterdam and was asking permission to join her son in London. Steengracht reported the manner of the Nuncio's approach in the following terms:

¶ The Nuncio called on me today and handed me a verbal note, with the immediate comment that this was a matter that was really outside his competence and that, if nothing could be done about it, he could readily resign himself to the fact.[4]

2 Memorandum by Woermann of Oct. 15, 1942, StS: V, AA, Bonn (MS).
3 Memorandum by Woermann, Nov. 6, 1942, ibid. (MS).
4 Memorandum by Steengracht, Aug. 5, 1943, ibid. (MS).

When Pius XII made his address to the Sacred College of Cardinals in June 1943, more than three million Jews had already been killed. The five gas chambers at Auschwitz had been put into operation.

No document known at present enables us to establish a definite link between the reserve maintained by the Holy See on the extermination of the Jews in late 1942 and in 1943, the evolution of the antireligious policy of the Germans and the international situation during the same period. Nevertheless, it is essential to consider the Jewish problem in the general context of the events that preoccupied the Vatican at that time. Such will be the object of the next two chapters.

Chapter VI

THE HOLY SEE AND
THE ANTIRELIGIOUS POLICY
OF THE REICH

1942–Summer 1943

1. The First Difficulties

Pius XII had hoped, upon his accession to the Supreme Pontificate, to arrive at a *modus vivendi* with the Reich which would put an end to the antireligious machinations of the government in Berlin. After the outbreak of war, these hopes were dashed by the increasingly severe measures adopted by the Germans in their treatment of the clergy and congregations in Poland.[1]

In the territory of the Reich itself, arbitrary decisions were aimed at the property of the Church. Thus, on November 28, 1940, Weizsäcker noted down the details of a talk he had just had with the Nuncio on the subject:

¶ Following the pattern of his last visit, the Nuncio today lodged with me a large number of complaints concerning the fact that, in the course of the current comprehensive re-

[1] See Chapters II and III.

settlement process, many Church institutions, monasteries, etc., had been sequestered or completely cleared out. The information reaching the Nuncio, from which he read to me for about a quarter of an hour, related to East Prussia and particularly to Silesia. Cardinal Bertram, he said, had written to the *Volksdeutsche Mittelstelle* [agency responsible for German populations living outside the Reich boundaries] on the 9th inst., to the Reich Leader of the S.S. [Himmler] on the 10th, and to Reich Minister Lammers on the 20th, without having received replies so far. The Nuncio asked me to use my influence to have the offices concerned answer Cardinal Bertram . . .[2]

When the campaign in Russia was launched, Hitler, probably wishing to avoid internal dissension, gave orders that the confiscation of ecclesiastical property be stopped. On July 7, 1941, Party Secretary Bormann addressed the following circular to all Gauleiters:

¶ The Führer has ordered:

Effective immediately and until further notice, all confiscation of ecclesiastical or monastic property is to cease. No independent action may be taken by Gauleiters in any circumstances, even when, in individual cases, special circumstances urgently require requisitioning of Church or monastery property on the basis of legal regulations. If, in any particular instance, a Gauleiter considers that such conditions exist, the matter must first be reported to the Führer and the report marked for my attention.[3]

In August, Msgr. Galen, Bishop of Münster, delivered

2 Memorandum by Weizsäcker, Nov. 28, 1940, StS: V, AA, Bonn (MS).
3 Führer Order (signed by Bormann), of July 7, 1941, ibid. (MS).

his famous sermons against the killing of the mentally sick. On September 30, the Director of the Vatican Affairs Department in the Ministry for Foreign Affairs made a note:

¶ In reply to my question whether any steps had been taken recently against the Bishop of Münster, the responsible official in the Ministry for Church Affairs informed me that, in view of the well-known sermons preached by the Bishop, the Ministry had proposed to the Reich Chancellery that the Bishop's endowment be withdrawn. In the past few days, however, the Führer had decided that for the time being no action be taken against the Bishop . . .[4]

The killing of mental patients also ceased. In conversation, Hitler indicated the same desire to be conciliatory, *for the duration of the war:*

¶ I have numerous accounts to settle, about which I cannot think today [he declared on October 25, 1941]. But that doesn't mean I forget them. I write them down. The time will come to bring out the big book! . . .

There's no sense in adding uselessly to the difficulties of the moment. One acts more shrewdly when one bides one's time. . . . When I read of the speeches of a man like Galen, I tell myself that there's no point in administering pinpricks, and that, for the moment, it's preferable to be silent.[5]

On December 13, the same theme:

¶ One day, the war will end. It will then be the final great task of my life to solve the religious problem. Only then will the German nation be secure.[6]

[4] Memorandum by Haidlen of Sept. 30, 1941, ibid. (MS).
[5] Adolf Hitler: *Hitler's Table Talk* (London: Weidenfeld and Nicolson; 1953), p. 90.
[6] Ibid., p. 140.

Yet during these same weeks, relations between the Vatican and the Reich worsened once again. Responsibility for this seems to have rested mainly on the shoulders of Alfred Rosenberg, one of the most fanatical enemies of the Catholic Church among the National-Socialist leaders, who had just been appointed as Minister responsible for the liberated territories in the East (Russia).

Catholic priests (with the exception of military chaplains) from the Reich or other countries were denied access to territories recently occupied.

Now the Church had hoped that it would be permitted to function in the territories won back from Bolshevism. It was believed in Berlin that for many years priests had been specially trained at the *Collegium Russicum* in Rome for eventual activity in liberated Russia.[7] But what seemed inadmissible to the Holy See was the exceptional treatment approved by the Germans in favor of the Orthodox clergy: at a time when authorization had not been given to a single civilian Catholic priest to enter the new territories, more than twenty Orthodox priests had already been admitted. On November 11, 1941, this was the subject of a vigorous complaint to Weizsäcker by the Nuncio.[8] At the Ministry for the Eastern Territories, it was explained to Weizsäcker that authority to enter had been granted to Orthodox priests only in a few exceptional cases. Catholicism, unlike the Orthodox faith, had never been the religion of those regions. For this reason, no justification was seen for activity on the part of the Catholic clergy.[9]

When direct approaches had proved fruitless, the Holy See made use of the good offices of Ambassador Attolico. On

---

[7] Memorandum by Haidlen, Oct. 15, 1941, StS: V, AA, Bonn (MS).
[8] Memorandum by Weizsäcker, Nov. 11, 1941, ibid. (MS).
[9] Memorandum by Fischer, Dec. 4, 1941, ibid. (MS).

November 29, he explained to his fellow diplomat von Bergen that the Reich would be well advised to give way on this particular point because the Russian question

¶ was the ground on which a rapprochement between the Reich and the Catholic Church could take place. The Church was a declared enemy of Bolshevism, and in the fight against Bolshevism, the interests of the Church and the Reich were identical. He anticipated that if the reports received in the Vatican [to the effect that Catholic priests were prohibited from entering the conquered territories] were corrected by the Reich, this would have a powerful effect, on the Pope above all.[1]

2. The Holy See and the Antireligious Policy of the Reich at the Beginning of 1942

THE SOVEREIGN PONTIFF in his Christmas message of December 24, 1941, made a clear reference to the persecution of the Church by the Germans.

On February 21, 1942, at the request of Berlin, Bergen sent an exhaustive analysis of the relations between the Reich and the Holy See.[2]

¶ The situation of the Roman Catholic Church in Germany, and the way relations between the Greater German Reich and the Holy See are shaping, remains the subject of the most lively and widespread interest in Catholic countries, particularly Italy and Spain. The latter countries radiate strong influence, with emotional overtones, toward South America. Scarcely a single diplomatic representative has so

[1] Telegram from Bergen to Berlin, Nov. 29, 1941, ibid. (MS).
[2] The most important passages in the Pope's address are quoted in Bergen's telegram.

far refrained from turning the talk to these topics and asking, more or less indiscreetly, for information—quite often
as soon as he has presented his credentials to the Pope during his inaugural visit. Ambassador Attolico, who died
recently, often talked with me about matters of Church
policy. He repeatedly informed me of complaints and fears
on the part of the Vatican, with the recognizable wish to
make a contribution to an improvement in German-Vatican
relations. Alfieri, his predecessor and present Ambassador
in Berlin, even on the occasion of the farewell visit he paid
me before departing for his new post, recommended me to
reach an early *modus vivendi* with the Curia, at least for
the duration of the war. In the course of that talk, he remarked that, regardless of the attitude of the individual and
of the state toward the Roman Church, no man of any
insight could overlook the fact of its power and far-reaching
influence or fail to see the advisability of peaceful co-
existence with it, particularly in the present difficult times.
I replied to the Ambassador that I, too, desired a settlement,
but that it appeared to me more appropriate to await the end
of the war and then to tackle the very extensive and intricate
complex of questions in an atmosphere of less tension and
greater calm. To deal with isolated questions beforehand
could only have a disturbing effect.

Bergen then emphasized that the Spanish diplomats, as
well as the diplomats of numerous other countries well disposed toward the Axis Powers, were watching developments
with concern. After briefly recalling the dangerous tension that
had developed between the Holy See and the Reich during the
Pontificate of Pius XI, the German Ambassador went on to
describe the main features of Pius XII's attitude.

¶ Soon after the present Pope ascended the throne, I pointed out that Pius XII, who in accordance with an old prophecy had been designated "Pater Angelicus," cherished a wish to go down in history as a "great Pope," in the style of Leo XIII—indeed, as the Pope who ushered in and consummated a peace based on justice, as the bringer of peace to the world. It was, I said, from this point of view, as well as others, that his first acts of authority should be judged.

Next, Bergen recalled the various steps to maintain peace which Pius XII undertook on the eve of the war [see Chapter I], among them his efforts to save the peace during the Polish crisis, at the price of the return of Danzig to the Reich, and his appeals for peace after the outbreak of hostilities, especially in his Christmas messages. The Ambassador then described the attitude of the Pope toward Germany, listed the pertinent telegrams which he sent in 1939, and continued:

¶ Pius XII has lived too long in Germany; has traveled too much to every corner of Germany and seen it all; knows the German language, German history and German ways too well; and has too many personal connections with the country to look upon the Germany of today with the eyes of a stranger and without understanding.

Even as the Nuncio in Germany, the present Pope worked toward creating clear and good relations between Church and State. If regulating relations between State and Church in Germany represented the life work of Nuncio and Cardinal Pacelli, then as Pius XII he will do his utmost to continue this life work, even if he has to transmute it into somewhat different forms.

Pius XII's friendly, perhaps even cordial, relations with

this or that man in public life in countries belonging to the group of powers that are hostile to Germany must not be taken as a reason for harboring distrust. The Holy See, and very specially the present Pope, will always be at pains to be on good terms, wherever possible, with all states. This is inherent in the supranational character of the Catholic Church. But for that very reason, it is a strict principle of Vatican diplomacy to keep questions of church policy entirely apart from politics and national and political antagonisms. In the Vatican, heavy emphasis is laid on the claim that this principle has always been strictly adhered to in respect of Germany. Pius XII will observe it with heightened conscientiousness. And there is no danger that any French influences may make themselves felt in the handling of the question of the German churches.

Bergen then recalled that the Holy See adopted a position of reserved neutrality vis-à-vis the various forms of government and cited the Pope's statements at the Eucharistic Congress in Budapest (a topic touched upon in a telegram of Bergen's quoted in Chapter I). The Ambassador went on to deal with the immediate causes of tension between the Holy See and the Reich and enumerated the long list of complaints made by the Vatican—from the suppression of confessional schools or of crucifixes in public buildings in Bavaria to the measures directed against the Church in Poland. Not until this point did Bergen quote the Pope's Christmas message. From this, the Ambassador reproduced the following passages:

¶ There is no place in the framework of a New Order, based on moral principles, for persecution of religion or of the Church. A living faith in a personal, transcendental God radiates a genuine and stalwart moral strength which gives form and direction to the whole. Faith, after all, is not merely a virtue: it is the divine portal by which any and every virtue gains access to the temple of the soul. It shapes firm and strong characters which stand fast amid temptations aimed at reason and justice. If this has always been true, how much more so must it be when a maximum of moral strength is demanded of all, from the leading statesman down to the last citizen; when the task is to build a new Europe and a new world on the ruins accumulated by this world war, with its violence, its hatred and its estrangements.

After going into the passage of the address which dealt with social questions, Bergen quoted the most important section of the papal message:

¶ God is Our witness how lovingly we embrace all peoples, without exception. To avoid even the semblance of partiality for one side, We have, so far, subjected Ourself to the utmost restraint. Yet the anti-religious measures and the objectives they pursue are such that We feel obliged in the name of truth to speak out, if only to counter possible confusion among those of Our own faith.

After this quotation, Bergen switched to commentary; he continued his telegram in these terms:

¶ It is known here that strong forces from various camps are constantly working to induce the Pope to make an ostentatious demonstration against us in the manner of his predecessor, explicitly naming Germany, the object being to expose and brand the alleged persecution of the Church in Germany. The reason given is the argument, which was advanced all too often under Pius XI, that silence on the part of the Pope would be interpreted as incomprehensible toleration, if not approval, and could not fail to wreak irremediable havoc in the consciences of countless numbers of the faithful. Cardinals and priests in the Pope's own entourage have a hand in these machinations. To the annoyance of many, the Pope so far has not yielded to this constant and growing pressure. Meanwhile, information reaching me indicates that the incessant lamentation about the situation of the Church and the faithful in Germany and the occupied areas depress the Pope profoundly, and that reports of intentions on the part of the Party, once the war is won, to launch a general offensive against the Church are causing him deep disquiet. It is said that, without abandoning his hopes for peace, he is beginning to take up defensive positions and prepare for eventual battle.

Moreover, in theory, the statements I have quoted on the subject of religion have general validity and would strike Bolshevism first. Meanwhile, Stalin's declarations about religious freedom in Russia, backed by propaganda and joyfully hailed by Roosevelt, have had a narcotic effect here, and the result has been that the permission granted to Polish Jesuits to go to Moscow on pastoral duty is being contrasted with the closing of the Ukraine by the Germans to Roman Catholic priests and the dismantling, allegedly by order, of crucifixes in Bavaria. There can be no doubt that the Pope's observations have a strong bearing on Germany and should be interpreted as an admonition or perhaps even as a warning to us.

Bergen next describes how greatly the religious persecution attributed to Germany is being exploited by enemy propaganda. Among the Italian prelates, who cannot forget that Germany is the land of the Reformation, this propaganda is not altogether without effect, and many of them are incapable of grasping at all "the extraordinary revitalization which the National Socialist idea represents." He ended the telegram with these words:

¶ Thus the Pope is perhaps the only individual among the leading personalities of the Church who is attempting to familiarize himself with the new Germany and to do it justice but who, as Supreme Pontiff, is unable to go beyond the limits set for him. Should the need arise, he will stand forth as the dauntless protector and champion of his Church but he will not develop into the great papal reformer for whom many devout Catholics even here, as they privately intimate, are yearning.

The experience of history teaches that state leaders of a nationalist turn of mind, when they assert and uphold the rights and vital interests of the peoples in their charge, of necessity become involved in conflict with the supertotalitarian, politically conscious papacy. The more self-assured and powerful the governments, the more violent are the effects of the clash. A comprehensive settling of accounts with the Holy See is inevitable and mandatory for us, once the war is over. But even in the event of our opting for a peaceful exchange of views with the Curia, which is still possible, it must be our aim not to strive for the revival of outmoded agreements on the lines of a concordat but to bring about a radical, all-embracing solution.[3]

Bergen's intention was clear: the German Ambassador wanted to avoid a sharpening of tensions, to prevent his government from adopting new anti-religious measures; and, if possible, to induce the National-Socialist leaders to withdraw

[3] Letter from Bergen to Berlin, Feb. 21, 1942, StS: V, AA, Bonn (MS).

measures already taken. To attain his objective, Bergen was making very skillful use of an impressive array of arguments: tension between the Reich and the Holy See, he declared, was perturbing Germany's allies, particularly the Italians and the Spaniards, and was serving its enemies as a first-rate propaganda weapon. This was one of the foreign policy arguments. The second was even more convincing: the Curia, Bergen intimated, could no longer make any absolute distinction between the Reich and the Soviet Union if antireligious measures in the Reich were intensified, while Moscow, by contrast, was permitting the development of a certain degree of religious liberty. They were thus gambling with the tacit support of the Catholic Church in the fight against Bolshevism; in February 1942, shortly after the German armies had suffered their first heavy reverses on the Eastern Front, this argument carried no small weight. To make his plea even more convincing, Bergen analyzed the attitude of the Pope with great shrewdness: the Ambassador did not deny that the Pope had been, and still was, Germanophile; but the anti-German forces in his entourage were growing stronger and, if the situation continued to deteriorate, the Pope, whose foremost duty was to defend the interests of the Church, might one day find himself compelled to take a stand against the Reich. The Christmas message had been a warning which must be heeded. Finally, to placate the enemies of the Church, Bergen, with an allusion to world history, indicated that the day for an all-out decision would of necessity come, but that it would be wise to await the end of the war before undertaking a comprehensive review of the relations between the Holy See and the Reich.

As we shall see, Bergen's plea remained without result.

On February 24, Weizsäcker had a discussion with Msgr. Orsenigo:

¶ I asked the Nuncio casually today how many Catholic priests there were in the Dachau concentration camp. He said that, having no contact with the concentration camp, he could only offer an estimate; he gave the figure as 700 priests.[4]

On March 3, 1942, Bishop von Preysing protested publicly in Berlin Cathedral against the persecution which the clergy and their flock were suffering. On the 10th, Weizsäcker complained to Orsenigo about the Bishop's action:

¶ I told the Nuncio quite openly that it had come to my ears that he had been present at the reading of the pastoral letter in St. Hedwig's Church.

The Nuncio thereupon assured me, credibly, that though he had been in that church on the Sunday in question, he had not been present during the sermon nor during the reading of the pastoral letter. He also had had no idea that the pastoral letter I was objecting to was to be read out. It was only afterwards that he had heard about the reading and read the text.[5]

In June 1942, following an inexplicable decision by the Führer, tension was aggravated.

3. Hitler's Order of June 1942 and its Consequences

On June 22, Weizsäcker notified Bergen of a new order by the Führer:

¶ The Führer has made the following decision on the question of Germany's relations with the Vatican and the Catholic Church:

[4] Memorandum by Weizsäcker, Feb. 24, 1942, ibid. (MS).
[5] Memorandum by Weizsäcker, March 10, 1942, ibid. (MS).

[160]

1. The Führer does not wish relations with the Catholic Church to be handled as an entity, or represented on a uniform basis, affecting the Reich as a whole.

2. Relations with the Vatican are maintained by Germany solely with regard to the old Reich, that is, the part of the Reich concerning which the Concordat of 1933 was signed.

3. Although the Concordat is obsolete on many points, the Führer considers it as being officially in existence.

4. The Vatican, by informing the German Government that it cannot recognize any political changes of territory for the duration of the war, has automatically excluded itself from an official connection with the territories annexed or occupied since September 1939. The Führer wishes, however, to have the same relationship established in regard to what was formerly Austria and the other territories annexed before September 1939.

5. The following will be the competent authorities in these areas:

    for Germany, the appropriate representatives of the Reich; for example, the Reich Protector, the Governor, the Reich Commissioner and the Reich Delegate (*Statthalter*); for the Church, the local representatives of the Church; for example, Cardinals, Bishops, etc.

    In these territories, therefore, no political or diplomatic links with the Vatican would be permitted. It follows from this that the Ministry for Foreign Affairs alone maintains a connection with the Vatican.[6]

---

[6] Telegram from Weizsäcker to Bergen of June 22, 1942, ibid. (MS). The note from the Curia of January 18, 1942, was not found in the Wilhelmstrasse files.

Weizsäcker then commented on the Führer's decision, the consequence of which was obvious: if the Nuncio in Berlin or the Curia in Rome approached representatives of the Reich in connection with happenings outside the old Reich, the German diplomats would be obliged to refuse to enter into such conversations. Weizsäcker emphasized, however, that in answering such questions from the Nuncio or the Curia, officials should not refer to the Führer's decision but should simply draw attention to the note from the Curia of January 18, 1942, stating that, for the duration of the war, the Curia did not intend to recognize territorial changes which had taken place in the interim; and that they should represent the refusal to negotiate on the questions raised as a logical consequence of that note. Church representatives of the regions outside the frontiers of the old Reich had no authority to negotiate as representatives of the Vatican with the local German authorities.

On July 4, the Führer gave his close associates a long explanation of the measure he had just taken:

¶ In the event of the retirement of our present representative at the Vatican, I am not at all of the opinion that we must give consideration to the choice of a replacement. Germany's relations with the Vatican are based on the Reich Concordat. However, at the time when the Concordat was concluded, it represented a continuation of concordats with the various states, so that when the states were absorbed into the German Reich, the state concordats actually lapsed. It is a fact that the state concordats have continued in force and that the Reich Concordat simply served to confirm and guarantee them. In my view, therefore, as a legal consequence of the abolition of the sovereign rights of the states, relations between ourselves and the Vatican have become redundant.

[162]

Having regard to the war, I have taken no practical steps to implement this concept. Equally, however, I have shown no disposition at all to be accommodating toward efforts on the part of the Vatican to extend the Concordat to the new territories of the Reich. The Saar territory, Sudetenland, Bohemia and Moravia, the Reich district of Danzig-West Prussia, the Warthegau, a large portion of Silesia, and Alsace-Lorraine today have no relations regulated by state treaty with the Vatican. In those areas, therefore, church affairs must be ordered on a purely regional basis. If the Nuncio approaches the Ministry for Foreign Affairs with a view to gaining any kind of influence in the new territories of the Reich, he must be sent about his business. It must be explained to him that in the absence of a special concordat the regulation of church affairs in those areas is solely a matter for the Reich Delegate (*Statthalter*) and the highest local official of the religious community in the area concerned. In actual fact, it would have been better if the Nuncio had obtained this information from Lammers. Unfortunately, however, the Foreign Ministry, in its constant urge to acquire new responsibilities in this matter which lies outside its jurisdiction, has let itself be outwitted. Now the Ministry must extricate itself as best it can.

As regards the development of relations between State and Church, it is thoroughly gratifying from our point of view that over almost half of the Reich matters can be arranged without the shackle of a central concordat, that is, region by region. This absence of uniform regulations is quite useful for us because it promotes the settlement of State-Church relations which we are striving to achieve. The Church is always intent on exploiting our weakest point. Should there be a settlement embracing the whole

Reich, the Church would want to use as a basis that one of the concordats corresponding most closely to its wishes; that is, it would want the whole Reich to be adjusted to the circumstances of the region which is ideologically most backward and which is, therefore, most favorable to our opponent. If, however, matters are regulated regionally, the *Gauleiters* can move forward step by step in line with our own notions, according to the extent to which the populations in their areas have been ideologically softened up . . .[7]

The underlying reasons which led Hitler to make his decision at that particular moment are difficult to understand. It is hardly likely that the Führer was moved only by the desire to react to the Vatican note of January 18, 1942, which declared that the Holy See could not recognize any changes of territory for the duration of the war. Hitler's decision is all the less understandable in that it was bound to provoke increasing tension between the Vatican and the Reich at the very moment when the outcome of the war seemed more uncertain than ever.

On Oct. 9, Bergen addressed the following telegram to Berlin:

¶ Msgr. Sericano, acting for Msgr. Tardini, the Under Secretary of State now on vacation, today summoned Counselor Menshausen and handed him a memorandum on behalf of Cardinal Secretary of State, remarking that it concerned religious conditions in Wartheland.

Menshausen replied briefly that he, Sericano, was surely aware of the communications made by State Secretary von

---

[7] Adolf Hitler: op. cit., Vol. II, pp. 187 f. Retranslated using the version by Henry Ticker in *Hitlers Tischgespräche im Führerhauptquartier, 1941–1942* (Stuttgart: Union Deutsche Verlagsgesellschaft; 1963), pp. 435 f.

Weizsäcker to the Nuncio which stated that, for the reasons given at the time, discussions with the Curia must be confined to matters relating to the old Reich, that is, to the territory of the Reich as it existed when the Concordat was concluded in 1933.

Translated into German, the memorandum, typed on a plain sheet with no heading, runs as follows:

"Religious conditions in the region designated as the 'Warthegau' have given rise for some considerable time to very serious, and constantly growing, concern. The episcopate there has, in fact, gradually been almost entirely eliminated; the lay brothers and members of monastic orders have been reduced to an altogether inadequate percentage (of their former numbers), having been to a large extent deported or expelled from the country; training of the clergy has been forbidden; Catholic education of the young is being obstructed to the utmost; the sisters have been scattered; insuperable difficulties have been put in the way of pastoral work; numerous churches have been closed; the Catholic intellectual and charitable institutions have been destroyed; and hands have been laid on Church property.

"In August and September 1941, the Apostolic Nuncio in Germany handed the Reich Minister for Foreign Affairs detailed memoranda demanding restoration in the Warthegau of the proper measure of freedom of worship. Notwithstanding this, as a result of Ordinance No. 246 of September 16, issued by the Reich Delegate there, the situation has deteriorated.

". . . Should the situation, as is feared, grow still worse in consequence of new measures by the Office of the Reich Delegate, the Holy See, acting in fulfillment of the obliga-

tions of its office, would find itself compelled to emerge from the attitude of reserve which it has so far maintained, and this it would do, however reluctantly.
Vatican, October 8, 1942."

. . . From the final remark in the memorandum, it may be anticipated that, in the event of further measures in the domain of the Church in the Wartheland, the Holy See will enter the public arena with appropriately worded protests of some kind. In this connection, I cannot fail to draw attention to the confidential information, submitted with due reserve, in Telegram 197 of July 29, 1942,[8] according to which the Pope is preparing an encyclical that is reported to contain allusions to religious conditions in Germany.[9]

This telegram constitutes a document of considerable importance. In a note to the representative of the Reich, the Cardinal Secretary of State let it be understood that the Vatican would abandon its reserve and make a public pronouncement against the antireligious measures adopted by the Germans in Poland. In the end, the Sovereign Pontiff was to refrain from making any public protest, but this did not detract from the fact that the threat had been uttered. Now this occurred in the autumn of 1942, at a time when information regarding the extermination of the Jews was reaching the Vatican. The possibility cannot be excluded that the Nuncio may have intervened with Hitler on the subject of the Jews during these same months or at the beginning of 1943, as we suggested when analysing the address made by Pius XII to the Sacred College of Cardinals in June 1943.

The Vatican Archives could enlighten us on this point

[8] This document has not been found.
[9] Telegram from Bergen to Berlin, Oct. 9, 1942, StS: V, AA, Bonn (MS).

since the Wilhelmstrasse Archives refer only to the interventions by Msgr. Orsenigo, the character of which we have already noted. Was it that Pius XII, realizing that his threat to make a protest over Poland had been fruitless, had reached the conclusion that no appeal to the Germans, public or private, would serve any purpose? Did he, consequently, consider it pointless to threaten the Nazis with a protest against the extermination of the Jews? If that were so, the phrases used in the address to the Sacred College could easily bear the following interpretation: "We begged for a return to justice and mercy (in the case of the Poles) and we found Ourself facing a door that no key could open. We saw from this that any protest, public or private, concerning the Jews could only cause even greater evils."

The threat by the Holy See seemed to make Ambassador von Bergen uneasy. On October 11, he reverted to the arguments he had deployed in his analysis of February 21.[1] On January 13, 1943, Ribbentrop replied:

¶ Your telegraphed report of October 12, 1942, suggested that at the time the Vatican was operating in diplomatic quarters, especially among the Italian and Spanish representatives, with a story to the effect that German measures applied during the past year had brought about increasing tension in German-Vatican relations. Although such assertions by the Vatican in no way correspond with the facts, I have so far refrained from instructing you to take any special diplomatic action to counter them. I thought it right to await further developments. In the meantime, it seems that the Vatican, too, has not deemed it appropriate to translate into deeds the statements it made then because no indication has

[1] Telegram from Bergen to Berlin, Oct. 11, 1942, ibid. (MS).

come to my knowledge of any attempt on the part of the Vatican to stir up feeling against us by claiming that there has been any deliberate sharpening of our attitude towards the Catholic Church. However, on this point, I request a report on your own observations. In any event, if, in future, the Vatican should again assert that German measures against the Catholic Church have led to a sharpening of tension in German-Vatican relations, I would ask you to take the strongest possible countermeasures and, in so doing, to make the following points orally:

1. Nothing has happened in Germany during the War that could be construed as deliberate German action aimed at aggravating our relations with the Vatican ...

2. If the Vatican wishes to see a sharpening of tension in the fact of our having limited diplomatic discussions with the Vatican to questions relating to the old Reich, then the Vatican itself has brought about this state of affairs by refusing, in its note of January 14, 1942, to recognize territorial changes that have occurred in recent years. The Government of the Reich has done nothing more than to draw the appropriate conclusions from this attitude on the part of the Vatican.

3. The restraint observed by German authorities shows clearly that there is no intention on our side to aggravate the situation vis-à-vis the Vatican. However, should the Vatican, for its part, threaten to undertake, or perhaps carry out, a political or propaganda campaign against Germany, the Government of the Reich would naturally be compelled to react accordingly. For this purpose, the Reich Government would lack neither effective material nor the possibility of taking concrete measures against the Catholic Church. The

Reich Government hopes that the need to apply such measures will not arise; rather, that the Vatican will be convinced that it is in the interests of both sides alike to avoid any aggravation or sharpening of tension in German-Vatican relations.[2]

Bergen's answer of January 15 did not indicate clearly whether the German Ambassador had brought his Minister's threats to the notice of his opposite numbers in the Curia. In his opinion, the Pope would do nothing to impair further the relations between the Holy See and the Reich so long as no German initiative compelled him, out of regard for the "obligations of his office," to abandon his reserve. Manifestly, the Ambassador was trying to calm Ribbentrop and to avoid a breach, whose consequences for the Church and for the Reich might be disastrous.[3]

On January 24, the Reich Minister for Foreign Affairs replied to the Ambassador:

¶ From your telegram No. 12 of January 15, I infer that, according to your observations, there are at present no indications that the Vatican is moving on a course that would aggravate its relations with the Reich. If this assumption is borne out, as was made clear in my instructions of January 13, no steps are contemplated on the German side which would worsen relations with the Vatican. If, however, you should detect any evidence that the Vatican is preparing to drop its reserve and take up a political or propaganda position hostile to Germany, it would have to be made aware beyond all doubt—and to direct attention to this was the main object of my instructions of January 13—that any

---

[2] Telegram from Ribbentrop to Bergen, Jan. 13, 1943, ibid. (MS).
[3] Telegram from Bergen to Ribbentrop, Jan. 15, 1943, ibid. (MS).

aggravation of relations between Germany and the Vatican would certainly not operate solely to the disadvantage of Germany but, rather, that the Reich Government would lack neither telling propaganda material nor opportunities for concrete action as an effective response to any blow aimed by the Vatican at Germany. I would ask you to keep this latter aspect of the matter constantly in mind so that it can be brought to bear at your end at the appropriate moment with all possible emphasis.[4]

In view of the Minister's unyielding attitude, Bergen pointed out on January 25 that, if the situation arose, Pius XII would not allow himself to be intimidated. He recalled a discussion he had had with Cardinal Pacelli in 1937, in the course of which the latter, while expressing a strong desire for an understanding, nevertheless declared that, in the event of a struggle between the Church and the Reich, the Reich would be the loser. Bergen then returned to the problems of the moment and added:

¶ Pius XII is no more amenable to threats than we are. If a fight should be forced on the Church, he anticipates that many more Catholics will lapse, but he is firmly convinced that the majority would stay and, cleansed in spirit, would remain true to their faith; and he is further convinced that the clergy, once aroused and steeled, would be prepared for extreme sacrifices. Despite this, as the harbinger of peace, he would prefer to avoid the fight, if only to spare millions of Catholics from grave conflicts of conscience. As against this, the Pope shows a high degree of understanding for objective reasoning and factual considerations and, therefore, if the circumstances arose, would not close his mind

[4] Telegram from Ribbentrop to Bergen, Jan. 24, 1943, ibid. (MS).

to the great significance of the underlying thought in your instructions of January 13, namely, that it is equally in the interests of both sides to avoid an aggravation or exacerbation of German-Vatican relations."[5]

The open breach, which the slightest German move henceforth might have provoked, did not take place. The Germans did not give up any of their positions and inflicted on the Holy See a defeat which, though only symbolic, nevertheless marked the end of the battle.

On March 18, Weizsäcker reported to Bergen about an incident which had just brought him into conflict with Nuncio Orsenigo:

¶ On March 15, Nuncio brought me sealed letter from Cardinal Secretary of State Maglione to the Reich Minister for Foreign Affairs.

I asked Nuncio to call on me today, returned the letter to him and, as instructed, made the following observations:

As the Reich Minister for Foreign Affairs was at the moment absent, I had opened the sealed letter given to me by him after Nuncio had left, and had seen that the content of this letter was concerned with the presentation of complaints relating to the Warthegau region and the General Government.

Weizsäcker once again explained to the Nuncio why the Reich Government was not prepared to discuss with the Vatican the territories outside the boundaries of the old Reich. In his report to Bergen, he then described how his conversation with the Nuncio proceeded. He told Orsenigo:

¶ As the present letter from the Cardinal Secretary of State simply ignored this communication and once again related

[5] Telegram from Bergen to Ribbentrop, Jan. 25, 1943, ibid. (MS).

solely to religious conditions in the Warthegau and in the General Government, I was not in a position to forward it to the Reich Minister of Foreign Affairs, but, instead, asked the Nuncio to take the letter back with him.

The Nuncio was greatly embarrassed by my statements. He believed that to accept the return of the letter would mean for him a personal defeat which would be very much held against him in Rome.

Msgr. Orsenigo then attempted to convince Weizsäcker that the letter did not represent an ordinary diplomatic document, such as he, as Nuncio, would have conveyed to the Secretary of State, but that it fell into the wider domain of the general activity of the Catholic Church. It constituted an indirect statement of the Pope's position which belonged on a higher level than that of normal diplomatic communications. Weizsäcker, with all the cards in his hand, was able to counter that if the Nuncio chose to present the letter on such terms, he would simply make the rebuff more serious.

¶ As matters stood now, the person of the Pope was unaffected and there was no refusal on the part of the Reich Minister for Foreign Affairs. What I was suggesting to him now was nothing more than the tacit withdrawal of the document, which in this way became nonexistent and, so far as outward appearances were concerned, no one would know anything about it . . .

The Nuncio withdrew the letter. He intimated to Weizsäcker that his days in Berlin probably "were now numbered." The Secretary of State ended his telegram by stressing that "matter was being handled here (in Berlin) under seal of deepest secrecy."

"In case you are questioned on the matter, please act as if you had no information."[6]

Msgr. Orsenigo remained at his post. It may be asked why, in this case, the Holy See displayed such unqualified moderation. Two theories suggest themselves. It is plausible to argue that, as in previous years, the Pope hesitated in the face of a trial of strength that might have led many German Catholics to turn away from Rome.

Another possibility cannot be excluded. This was in the spring of 1943; the Allies had landed in North Africa in 1942 and the German forces in Tunisia were soon to surrender. Above all, the armies of the Reich had capitulated at Stalingrad. From now on, the defeat of Germany was a reasonable prospect; a victorious thrust by the Russians into Eastern and Central Europe, foreseeable. The German documents which we shall quote in the next chapter give the impression that, in the Vatican's view, the Bolshevik danger would henceforth override every other consideration and that, since Germany was the sole rampart against the specter of Bolshevism, nothing must be done to weaken the Reich.

[6] Telegram from Weizsäcker to Bergen, March 18, 1943, ibid. (MS). Cf. the description of this incident in Ernst von Weizsäcker: *Erinnerungen* (Munich: Paul List Verlag; 1950), pp. 352 f.

Chapter VII

THE DEVELOPMENT OF THE INTERNATIONAL SITUATION AND THE BOLSHEVIK THREAT, 1942–1943

FROM THE SPRING of 1943, fear of a Bolshevization of Europe seemed to dominate the political thinking of the Holy See. Yet Pius XII never took up a public stance against the Soviet Union. Religious persecution in the countries under German rule was one probable reason for his attitude; the possible reactions of the peoples under the German yoke and the reactions of the Allied nations was another.

The first fears of the Vatican were made manifest when it became apparent that the Reich would not succeed in defeating the Soviet Union.

1. The Russian Resistance, 1942

ON APRIL 1, 1942, Bergen wrote:

¶ I learn in confidence . . . that in connection with the article appearing in the *Critica fascista* No. 8 of February 15, 1942, under the title "The Church And The World Crisis," which reproached the Vatican for failing to take a stand against

Bolshevism, Cardinal Pizzardo told the Italian Ambassador that the Vatican would very gladly take up a position against Bolshevism, but could not do so in existing circumstances without also taking account of events in Germany. On the other hand, as the Church did not wish to bring up these matters out of consideration for Germany, there could also be no (public) stand against Bolshevism.[1]

But however great the Vatican's reticence might be with regard to taking an official position, its options would be determined by the fundamental attitude it had adopted. Its silence on the subject of "what was going on in Germany" would be dictated by the need to preserve the indispensable bastion against Russian expansion now represented by the Third Reich.

On December 27, 1942, Bergen went to the Pope to proffer New Year's wishes, and was received in private audience. That same day he reported to Weizsäcker the main points of his interview with the Pope:

¶ After I had conveyed the New Year wishes, as instructed, and the official portion of the audience was over, Pope kept me back for a rather lengthy private conversation. Pope, of his own accord, avoided bringing in political questions or matters of Church policy, and indicated his assent to remarks of mine scattered through the conversation only by appropriate gestures: for example, in response to my reference to the historic significance of the heroic German struggle in the East; the danger of Bolshevism to which the British and the Americans wanted to expose Europe; the absurdity of Stalin's proclamation of religious freedom, and

---

[1] Telegram from Bergen to Berlin, April 1, 1942, StS: V, AA Bonn (MS).

so on. The Pope expressed explicit approval when I alluded to Raphael's well-known fresco "Attila defied by Pope Leo the Great" and contended that Stalin's hordes, unlike Attila's horsemen, would certainly not bypass Rome but, rather, would spare neither St. Peter's nor the Vatican City.[2]

2. *The Aftermath of Stalingrad*

On January 31, 1943, the German armies of Marshal Paulus capitulated at Stalingrad. At the Vatican, it was realized that the Axis Powers now might lose the war. On March 10, Weizsäcker recorded a talk he had just had with the Finnish Minister:

¶ The Finnish Minister today told me excerpts from talks he has had with his colleague Griepenberg, the Finnish Minister to the Vatican.

Griepenberg said that the prevailing view in the Vatican was that the strength of the Axis Powers was going downhill faster than that of the opposing side. Time, therefore, was not working for the Axis.[3]

From this moment, it seemed to be in the interest of the Vatican to try to bring about a separate peace between the Western Allies and the Axis. Certainly, such an eventuality had become highly dubious since the Allied declaration of January 27, 1943, demanding the unconditional surrender of the Axis Powers and Japan. Yet, to the Holy See, such a separate peace may have seemed even more necessary because from the beginning of the year there had been reason to believe that secret contacts were in progress between the Germans and the Russians:

[2] Telegram from Bergen to Weizsäcker, Dec. 27, 1942, ibid. (MS).
[3] Memorandum by Weizsäcker, March 10, 1942, ibid. (MS).

¶ It is rumored in Vatican quarters," wrote Bergen on May 4, "that confidential peace soundings have taken place in Switzerland in the last few months between representatives of the Reich and of Soviet Russia.

The discussions are said to have broken down as a result of exorbitant Russian demands. Thus, for example, it is reported that Russia has claimed Bessarabia and Upper Silesia, as well as the portion of Poland it had occupied. It is alleged that the soundings have now been resumed on a new basis proposed by Germany.[4]

These rumors were partially correct. The contacts took place not in Switzerland but in Sweden, where the Japanese Colonel Uchigawa and Mme Alexandra Kollontai, the Ambassadress of the Soviet Union in Stockholm, acted as intermediaries. On the German side, Ribbentrop was the prime mover in seeking these soundings, unbeknown, it seems, to Hitler.

The Holy See was probably ignorant of the precise details of the Russo-German contacts of early 1943, but the prospect of a new Russo-German pact, however vague that prospect might be, could not but act as a spur to all efforts aiming at an arrangement between the Reich and the Western Powers.

The details we possess up to now of the attempts at mediation by the Holy See in 1943 are confused. Accordingly, we shall refrain here from reproducing the very contradictory reports on the subject, but will confine ourselves to sifting out indications that point to the probable intentions of the Vatican.

On May 19, 1943, Dino Alfieri, the Italian Ambassador in Berlin, had a talk with Steengracht, the new German State Secretary, who had just replaced Weizsäcker (soon to take

---

[4] Telegram from Bergen to Berlin, May 4, 1943, ibid. (MS).

over his new post as Ambassador to the Vatican). Alfieri, who himself had been Italian Ambassador to the Holy See, had continued to maintain very close contacts with the Curia. After mentioning the Klessheim meeting between the Führer and the Duce, the Italian diplomat went on to speak of the "European idea."

¶ . . . Further, Alfieri again came back, of his own accord, to to the European idea and stressed that it must be possible to strengthen the anti-Bolshevik front by some sort of declaration about the future fate of the peoples of Europe. Moreover, he was convinced that it would not be difficult to win from the Pope a gesture which would amount to aid in strengthening an anti-Bolshevik front. In this respect, the only thing he would consider necessary would be that we suspend temporarily certain measures inside the country which the Church interpreted as being directed against itself.

I replied to the Ambassador that in this respect nothing had changed since our last conversation and that we were gathering all our strength to inflict a decisive defeat on the Bolsheviks. I feared that a gesture on the part of the Pope might be understood in the sense of our being inclined to make peace, whereas he was, of course, aware of our standpoint, which called for victory without compromise.

Alfieri replied that he had not been talking of a peace gesture by the Pope but had meant that not the least of the Pope's attributes was that of a warm-hearted Italian patriot, and that the Holy Father had, as he had often put into words in his (Alfieri's) company, great sympathies for Germany. In order to facilitate the Axis struggle, he would certainly respond to an appropriately phrased suggestion by helping to mobilize the anti-Bolshevik forces of Europe.[5]

On July 5, the new Ambassador of the Reich to the Holy See, former State Secretary Ernst von Weizsäcker, presented his credentials to Pius XII. After the ceremony, the Sovereign Pontiff granted Weizsäcker a private audience which the latter reported in the following terms:

¶ After the Pope had commissioned me to convey his greetings and wishes to the Führer and had mentioned the visit to the Vatican of the Reich Minister for Foreign Affairs, he dealt in our dialogue mainly with three topics:

1. *His gratitude for the years he had spent in Germany as Nuncio* and his unchanged affection for Germany and the German people.

2. *The relationship between Germany and the Vatican.* In this connection, the Pope spoke first of the fact that the Reich Concordat had come about because Germany had wanted it. Unhappily, conditions had later crystallized which seemed to obstruct for an indefinite period the treatment of, and solutions for, outstanding questions between Germany and the Vatican. I confirmed that this viewpoint, dispassionately stated, corresponded to my own. Naturally, the Pope hopes for a resolution of present difficulties at a later date.

3. *The general situation.* This topic afforded me an opportunity to lay proper emphasis on the German effort against Bolshevism. The Pope spoke of his own experiences with the Communists in Munich in 1919.

[5] Memorandum by Steengracht, May 19, 1943, StS: Italien, AA, Bonn (MS).

He condemned the mindless formula of our opponents demanding "unconditional surrender." At the same time, he expressed the view that there was, at present, no lead on which to base any kind of practical work for peace. I added that my government did not expect anything of the kind.

The conversation, which lasted about half an hour, was conducted by the Pope without visible passion but with an undertone of spiritual fervor which was transformed into a recognition of common interests only when the discussion turned to the handling of the fight against the Bolsheviks.

It has been agreed that the content of the conversation shall be regarded as completely confidential."[6]

The importance of this document is obvious. The Pope, it suggested, had let it be understood for the first time that a community of interest existed between the Vatican and Germany in the fight against Bolshevism.

3. The Allied Landing in Sicily and the Problem of Protecting Rome

THE THREAT of Communism remained and, as we shall see, continued to be the main preoccupation of the Holy See. That does not mean, however, that we can pass over in silence all the worry that was occasioned in the Vatican by the extension of the combat zone to Italian soil as well as by the threat of massive bombardment that hung over the Eternal City. Moreover, these problems were indirectly linked with the fear of Communism, for the chaos and misery that might be caused by fighting and bombardment could not fail to foster the spread

[6] Telegram from Weizsäcker to Berlin, July 5, 1943, StS: V, AA, Bonn (MS).

of extreme left-wing movements among the population of the country. But over and above this, the Vatican was concerned to preserve close relations with both Allies and Germans in order to persuade the belligerents to spare Rome so far as was humanly possible. Here, too, the Holy See felt obliged to take into account the necessity to maintain as correct as possible a footing with the Reich in order to secure German acceptance of the conditions demanded by the Western Allies as the price of avoiding the bombardment of Rome.

On May 13, 1943, the Axis forces in Tunisia capitulated. On July 10, the Allies landed in Sicily. That same day, Roosevelt sent a message to the Pope:

¶ By the time this reaches your Holiness a landing in force by American and British soldiers will have taken place on Italian soil. Our soldiers have come to rid Italy of Fascism and all its unhappy symbols, and to drive out the Nazi oppressors who are infesting her soil . . .[7]

According to Weizsäcker, the message from the American President was not welcome at the Holy See. On July 12, the German Ambassador wrote to Berlin:

¶ The telegram from Roosevelt to the Pope in connection with the landing of American troops in Sicily has aroused little joy in the Vatican. An Undersecretary of State in the Vatican told me today that this telegram, and particularly its publication by the American agencies, represented a propaganda procedure which was no less reprehensible for being a matter of repetition. Obviously, any reaction to it was out of the question.[8]

[7] *Keesing's Contemporary Archives*, London, p. 5866.
[8] Telegram from Weizsäcker to Berlin, July 12, 1943, StS: V, AA, Bonn (MS). The American documents likewise reveal the embarrassment that was caused in the Holy See by Roosevelt's message (telegram

On July 14, Weizsäcker dealt at greater length with the atmosphere in the Vatican after the Allied landing in Sicily:

¶ One might have believed that, as the battle zone drew nearer on Italian soil, some emotion would become perceptible in the Vatican, too. There is, however, almost no sign of this, at least no outward sign. The semi-official Vatican newspaper is making a point of refraining from publishing any communiques on the military situation. It is pushing this abstention so far that it has, as yet, not printed a single word about the fighting in Sicily.

Naturally, even the Vatican cannot regard these events with indifference. No amount of argument will alter the fact that the hierarchy of the Church, at its apex, is almost entirely Italian and, for the most part, feels accordingly. And Roosevelt's propagandist telegram of last Saturday did nothing to change this . . . During a private audience which I had, in company with my wife, last Sunday, that is, on the day after the Anglo-American landing, the Pope, in a reference to Sicily, used the word "concern," although, it is true, he then immediately changed the subject.[9]

On July 19, the day of Hitler's meeting with Mussolini at Feltre, Rome underwent its first bombardment. It would be outside the scope of our subject to report here the countless approaches made by the Vatican to both Allies and Germans with the object of sparing the Italian capital from the fate of Germany's principal cities.[1] So far as the Germans were con-

---

from Tittmann to Hull of July 12, 1943, *FRUS* 1943 II, p. 928); however, Pius XII confined himself in his reply to the American President to stressing the neutrality of the Vatican (ibid., p. 931).

[9] Telegram from Weizsäcker to Berlin, July 14, 1943, ibid. (MS).

[1] The reader can find much detail on this point in the memoirs of Raffaele Guariglia: *Ricordi 1922–1946* (Naples: Edizioni Scientifiche Italiane; 1950), p. 506 and *passim*. See also *FRUS*, 1943, II, pp. 910 f.

cerned, the aim of the Curia was to secure the evacuation of command posts located in the suburbs of the city, particularly the headquarters of Field Marshal Albert Kesselring. These efforts only partially achieved their objective. But regardless of their success, they were, at that time, one more reason for the Holy See to avoid a head-on clash with the Germans.

4. The Fall of Mussolini, the Badoglio Government and the Separate Italian Armistice, July 25–September 3, 1943

ON JULY 23, 1943, after more than twenty years in power, Mussolini was stripped of his functions by the King, then arrested. Elements hostile to the Duce within the Fascist Grand Council, acting in conjunction with the Court and part of the Army, brought off this astonishing coup d'état without a fight. The Fascist Government collapsed in the course of a single day. It is known that, through the medium of Alcide De Gasperi, the Vatican was at least aware of the plans of one of the groups hostile to the Duce,[2] but no document exists that would warrant the suggestion that the Holy See had in any way encouraged or obstructed the conspiracy.

The King named Marshal Pietro Badoglio to head the new government. The latter made a proclamation saying that Italy would continue to fight at the side of the Reich, but from the moment of his accession to power he endeavored, in concert with the King and the members of his cabinet, to extricate Italy from the war.

On July 27, Weizsäcker reported first reactions from the Vatican:

[2] F. W. Deakin: *The Brutal Friendship* (New York: Harper & Row; 1963), p. 241. Alcide De Gasperi was to become Premier of the Republic of Italy.

¶ As late as Sunday, it had not been believed in the Office of the Secretary of State in the Vatican that the Duce would abandon the fight. Now that matters have reached this pass, the Vatican, after the event, is showing more respect than is Rome itself for the Duce, particularly as the signatory of the Lateran Treaties of 1929. The change (of regime) is regarded as an event of the most far-reaching significance.

I have just been with Cardinal Secretary of State Maglione . . . The Cardinal questioned me with interest about German reaction to the events in Rome. I replied that the war was taking its course regardless of these domestic happenings in Italy. As we talked, it was easy to see that the Cardinal did not seriously believe in Badoglio's formula that "the war will go on."

On the other hand, Maglione assured me that he has so far had no direct communication from the new Italian government. He told me he had now summoned Blasco Lanza d'Ajeta [Ciano's Chief of Staff] to find out what the Government was thinking. I presume he does not wish to see Ciano himself.

The Cardinal said that, unless invited to do so by the Italian Government, neither he nor the Pope would take any steps in the direction of peace. In any case, Italy, of course, would have to take Germany into consideration.

The attitude of the Curia can probably be accurately read from these remarks by Maglione. The Curia desires peace. It would be glad to have peace dictated by moderation and in that event it would gladly provide its good offices. It believes that the path to this, which hitherto has been closed, may be opened by the Duce's departure.[3]

[3] Telegram from Weizsäcker to Berlin, July 27, 1943, StS: V, AA, Bonn (MS).

In actual fact, the reports concerning the policy desired, if not practised, by the Holy See during the ephemeral existence of the Badoglio Government are, taken as a whole, not at all clear. Communism was seen throughout as the main enemy, but there was hesitation as to the best means of fighting it. A separate armistice signed by Italy would weaken the Reich; on the other hand, to let Italy remain at war was to risk that this would favor the spread of Communism in the peninsula. In spite of these problems, certain of the German reports might convey the impression, as will be seen later, that in August 1943 the Holy See had worked out some very precise plans.

On July 31, the German Ambassador in Paris transmitted the following information to the Wilhelmstrasse:

¶ According to a report from Minister von Krug, President Laval told him, on the strength of a conversation between one of his colleagues and Nuncio Valerio Valeri, that it is possible to discern a stronger inclination in Vatican quarters to lead the Axis Powers and the Anglo-Americans toward a rapprochement, for the purpose of combatting Bolshevism. This development (he says) dates from the day Rome was bombed.

On the subject of the conversation in question, Minister von Krug has further learned that the Nuncio was asked by Laval's colleague whether the Pope still considered co-operation with Bolshevik Russia to be possible and was working toward this. The Nuncio thereupon replied spontaneously that co-operation between Russia and the Vatican had been put back a thousand years. The Pope, he said, was disturbed about the possibility of a Soviet-Russian victory and was using all the means at his disposal to pave the way for peace between Germany and England. In doing so, he hoped England might recognize that it was, in the final analysis, a European power and responsible for the survival of Christian culture in Europe.[4]

On August 3, Weizsäcker referred in a telegram to a letter from Undersecretary of State Montini which has not been found. The Ambassador wrote in particular:

¶ . . . It is clear that the letter from Undersecretary of State Montini reflects certain views held in the Vatican. In the Vatican, the situation of Italy is considered to be highly dangerous. There is no longer any belief in a victory for Italy or, consequently, for the Axis. It would be in accordance with Vatican wishes to have Italy "come out of the war well."

It is, in fact, Bolshevism that is the greatest cause of concern. The Pope included a warning against Bolshevism in his address to the Italian workers on June 13. The Church authorities had the address distributed in handbill form in the Communist-infected factories. I would further remind you of the public warnings, reported earlier, of the Archbishop of Milan, Cardinal Schuster.

I hear that the Vatican has in its possession extensive material on the recent upsurge of Communist propaganda among all strata of the population, even soldiers, which aims at a seizure of power by the proletariat.[5]

Without knowledge of the text of the letter from Msgr. Montini to which Weizsäcker alluded, it seems possible to infer from the first sentence of the telegram that the Undersecretary

---

[4] Telegram from Schleier to Berlin, July 31, 1943, StS: V, AA, Bonn (MS).
[5] Telegram from Weizsäcker to Berlin, Aug. 3, 1943, StS: Italien, AA, Bonn (MS).

of State was one of those who supported the view that Italy should negotiate a separate armistice.

As to the rapid spread of Communist agitation, the news sent by Weizsäcker was to a large extent correct. In fact, activity by the Communist Party of Italy had become evident since the reappearance of the newspaper *L'Unità* in June 1942. In March 1943, the Communists in Turin organized a vast strike movement, and from the moment the Fascist Government vanished from the scene, their influence in the industrial cities of Northern Italy rapidly increased.

On August 4, Weizsäcker reported some additional elements in the Vatican attitude to the Badoglio Government:

¶ ... For reasons of domestic policy, however, the Vatican is showing reserve toward the Badoglio Cabinet. The so-called freedom which it promises has opened so wide a path to Communist agitation that printed handbills against the Church and the Pope have been distributed in Rome. One such leaflet, which I have held in my hand, jeered at the Pope's manifestation of sympathy, after the event, for the victims of the American air attack on Rome, and criticized the Pope (i.e., Pius XI, the present Pope's predecessor), who had called Mussolini the man appointed by Providence etc. . . .

The fact is that the Church today is perturbed; to the Church, the archenemy, at home and abroad, is Communism and so it will remain. I have been assured that the American Government has been warned by the Vatican not to exert undue pressure on Italy, lest the unstable Badoglio Government slide leftward. As for the British Government, a close political collaborator of the Pope assured me that England is thoroughly aware of the danger from Soviet

Russia, only today it cannot yet publicly acknowledge this conviction.[6]

On August 18, a new telegram from Paris brought information which Minister von Krug had learned "from a reliable source." He wrote:

¶ 1. Archbishop of Paris, Cardinal Suhard, has expressed wish to visit Pope to urge that German Army and Church is only possible pillar protecting Europe from Communism. Everything must, therefore, be done to help German Army in the East to victory.

2. Vatican is presently endeavoring to bring about not only armistice but also peace between Western Allies and Italy. Prerequisite would be nonoccupation of Italy by Western Allies and freedom of German troops to withdraw. Such a peace is to be first step to union between Allies and Germans to create European-American-Christian united front against Asia.[7]

Von Krug's information was confirmed by a telegram from Lisbon of August 24:

¶ The Portuguese Ambassador to the Vatican, Carneiro Pacheco, has arrived in Lisbon and has been received by the Cardinal Patriarch. I learn in strict confidence that he brought him a message from the Cardinal Secretary of State which deals with the revival of Catholic Action in favor of peace and culminates in an appeal to the Portuguese clergy to combat Communism in the press and with all other means at their command . . .

[6] Telegram from Weizsäcker to Berlin, Aug. 4, 1943, StS: V, AA, Bonn (MS).
[7] Telegram from Schleier to Berlin, Aug. 18, 1943, ibid. (MS).

I am told further that Ambassador Pacheco reported that the Pope, through his representatives in England and America, is trying his utmost to achieve an arrangement by which Italy will be granted an honorable peace, on the basis that both belligerents quit Italian soil. He hopes that this will be the case by September and that from this a Western alliance against anarchy and Bolshevism will develop.[8]

The fact that information from Paris and from Lisbon coincided conveys the impression that for a while the Vatican hoped to induce the Western Allies and the Germans to reach an accord for a "demilitarization" of Italy and then, on the basis of that partial accord, to initiate a rapprochement on a much broader scale which would lead to a coalition of the Western Powers against Soviet Russia.

The matching information supplied by the German documents is confirmed in part by a report sent in July 1944 to a London prelate by his correspondent in the Vatican. According to that report, Pius XII is said to have dispatched one of his close collaborators, the architect Enrico Pietro Galeazzi, on a mission to New York late in August 1943 to persuade the American Government, through the medium of Cardinal Francis J. Spellman, to show understanding toward Germany and so prepare the ground for a rapprochement between the Allies and the Reich.[9]

At the same time, the Holy See is said to have defined yet again its attitude toward the Reich and the Soviet Union in an extremely important document which, according to Ambassador Weizsäcker, came to his knowledge "by chance" in September, but which had probably been written in July or August when the Badoglio Government was still functioning:

[8] Telegram from Huene to Berlin, Aug. 24, 1943, ibid. (MS).
[9] Document published by the *Journal de Genève* on July 27, 1964.

[189]

¶ By chance, I have been able to take a look at three documents which are characteristic of the Pope's political attitude, All three documents are dated after July 25 [the date of the fall of Mussolini].

The first contains an intervention with the Badoglio Government by the Curia on behalf of persecuted former Fascists. In the second, the Curia, acting on instructions from the Pope, intercedes on behalf of the Duce and his family, actually enumerating some twenty members of the family by name. It is worth noting that the names of Count Ciano and Edda Ciano are missing from among these.

The third document is particularly interesting. It contains an exposition by Cardinal Secretary of State Maglione to the Italian Government of the dangers threatening the world. Maglione says that the fate of Europe depends on the victorious resistance by Germany on the Russian front. The German Army is the only possible bulwark—*"baluardo"* —against Bolshevism. Should this bulwark break, European culture would be finished.[1]

Cardinal Maglione's note would seem to confirm that, from then on, the Holy See took the view that victorious resistance by the German armies in the East was essential for the safeguarding of Europe. Once again, only the Vatican Archives could enlighten us as to the exact phrasing of the note in question.

An impressive number of the German documents that I have quoted, and shall quote, underpin the argument which the Cardinal Secretary of State is said to have expounded to the Italian Government.

The Pope's intervention on behalf of Mussolini and some

[1] Telegram from Weizsäcker to Ribbentrop, Sept. 23, 1943, StS: V, AA, Bonn (MS).

members of his family is itself not without interest. Ciano had been the Ambassador of Italy to the Vatican from the beginning of 1943. During that period, he seems to have tried to establish contact with the Allies with a view to arranging a separate armistice for Italy and to have prepared the plot against Mussolini. In spite of this, the fact of his long collaboration with Mussolini—he was the Duce's son-in-law—would scarcely have sheltered him from possible action by the Badoglio Government,[2] so that intervention by the Pope on his behalf would have had its uses. The fact that the Sovereign Pontiff refrained from so intervening may have indicated by implication that the Holy Father condemned Ciano's political and diplomatic activities during the months of his tenure at the Vatican.

On September 3, Weizsäcker sent Berlin an even more explicit memorandum concerning Pius XII's political attitude:

¶ I continually receive proof how very much annoyed Vatican people are over Anglo-American policy, the spokesmen of which are regarded as clearing the path for Bolshevism. Concern in the Vatican about the fate of Italy and of Germany, too, is growing. A diplomat who enjoys special connections with the Vatican assured me yesterday Pope sternly condemns all plans aimed at weakening the Reich. A bishop working in the Curia told me today that in the Pope's view a powerful German Reich is quite indispensable for the future of the Catholic Church. From confidential transcript of conversation between an Italian political publicist and Pope, I gather that Pope, in reply to question as to what he

---

[2] Ciano's attitude was to remain ambiguous to the end. After Badoglio took power, Ciano tried to leave Italy. In late August, Badoglio contemplated arresting him, as was being demanded by many anti-Fascists. It was then that Mussolini's son-in-law accepted the "protection" of the Germans that cost him his life.

thought of the German people, replied: "They are a great nation who, in their fight against Bolshevism, are bleeding not only for their friends but also for the sake of their present enemies." It was the same attitude that prompted the Pope, in his address of September 1, to warn and criticize the Anglo-Americans. Core of the address is unmistakably directed at our Western opponents."[3]

On the very day when Weizsäcker sent his dispatch, the Italians signed a secret armistice with the Allies; on September 8, the American radio announced its terms. On the 9th, the first of the German troops entered Rome.

5. *The First Weeks of the German Occupation of Rome*

IN THE VATICAN, the necessity for an occupation of the Eternal City by the forces of the Reich was certainly regretted; but through it the Communist danger had been exorcized, for the moment at least, in that part of Italy that was now to be under German domination. The attention of the Holy See was now, therefore, directed mainly at Eastern Europe. On September 24, Weizsäcker wrote:

¶ It is interesting that, from the political point of view, the events in Italy, which are happening before everybody's eyes, are not being taken so seriously here as those on the Eastern Front. It is feared in the Vatican that, under the weight of events in the East, Germany might, in the end, throw itself into the arms of the Russians. The contention

[3] Telegram from Weizsäcker to Berlin, Sept. 3, 1943, StS: V, AA, Bonn (MS). Apparently, Weizsäcker was exaggerating the significance of the Pope's address. Pius XII demanded, as he had done before, a swift return to a peace dictated by moderation. Cf. *Acta Apostolicae Sedis*, 1943, p. 279. Of course, this call was incompatible with the Allies' demand for unconditional surrender.

that the German Government and the Russian Government are already in touch with one another cannot be eradicated.

Just as persistent is the Vatican's dream that the Western Powers will realize in time where their real interest lies and, will join the German effort to help save European culture from Bolshevism.[4]

On September 24, too, Nuncio Orsenigo expressed to State Secretary Steengracht the necessity for common action by the Reich and the Vatican against Communism:

¶ The Nuncio sought me out today [wrote Steengracht on September 24] and, of his own accord, turned the conversation to the sad conditions into which Italy had fallen since Badoglio's capitulation, and then began to talk about the danger of Communism to the world in general. I told him about the armed Communist bands which had been formed in Milan and Turin and impressed upon him that only swift action on our part could avert Bolshevik chaos in Upper Italy.

The Nuncio then declared, of his own accord, that in his view only Germany and the Vatican were in a position to tackle the Bolshevik peril, the former in the material, the latter in the spiritual, sphere. He went on to say that what Stalin was now doing with the Orthodox Church by installing a Bishop was absolute humbug and a crudely perpetrated swindle. It was only too regrettable that all sorts of functionaries in denominations other than the Catholic Church were being designated as Bishops and that the title of Bishop was in this way being degraded.[5]

Some days later, Weizsäcker himself reported on the

---

[4] Telegram from Weizsäcker to Berlin, Sept. 24, 1943, StS: V, AA, Bonn (MS).
[5] Memorandum by Steengracht, Sept. 24, 1943, ibid. (MS).

Vatican's negative reaction to Stalin's measures favoring religion:

¶ Stalin's new church policy, like the dissolution of the Comintern some time ago, is assessed in the Vatican as an act of political opportunism inspired by the Western Allies and one which can be rescinded from one day to the next. The Vatican's basic attitude of hostility toward the Soviet Union is unaffected by Stalin's church policy. Moreover, this policy runs counter to Rome's desires in regard to recatholicization in Russia.[6]

On October 3, the Germans learned that in the Vatican view there was a danger that the Russian offensive in the Balkans might be carried to a victorious conclusion.[7] On the 8th, Weizsäcker once again tried to summarize the main features of the political options before the Holy See, in the face of a world situation which was growing more and more menacing:

¶ 1. I should like to quote characteristic elements from conversations which I have had recently with foreign policy specialists in the Vatican.

A day or two after July 25, I asked Msgr. Tardini, the Undersecretary of State:

"What would you do now if you were Badoglio?"

Tardini: "I should not have accepted the post at all."

I: "But what if I were now to appoint you to it?"

Tardini: "Then I should resign."

Another said that the Badoglio Ministry was made up of Freemasons. No one could tell how far to the left they would land us.

[6] Telegram from Weizsäcker to Berlin, Sept. 28, 1943, ibid. (MS).
[7] Telegram from Moellhausen, Oct. 3, 1943, ibid. (MS).

Yet another priest (Jesuit) told me that the Church had fared well under Fascism. In the last few years in Italy, the Church had had things almost too easy in its fight against Communism.

I have already reported that the Pope is interceding with the Badoglio Government for decent treatment for the Duce and his family. He has also urged leniency for persecuted Fascists.

Since September 8, the gentlemen in the Vatican—who are, of course, almost all Italians—show embarrassment when the talk turns to their countryman Badoglio. A Vatican prelate said to me this last day or so: "Badoglio has covered us with shame."

"After the [fall?] of the Duce and again later after Badoglio's betrayal, Cardinal Secretary of State Maglione told me that he would be glad to do something for peace, but never for Italy alone, just as he would not do anything for Germany alone without the consent of Japan. Curia could not have a hand in the dissolution of our alliance. British publications proved (he said) that the Curia had had no part in Badoglio's armistice negotiations.

I need not quote anti-Bolshevik utterances. They come to my ears every day.

2. Hostility to Bolshevism is, in fact, the most stable component of Vatican foreign policy. Anything that serves the fight against Bolshevism is welcome to the Curia. The Anglo-American link with Soviet Russia is detested by the Vatican. The Holy See considers it pigheaded of them to persist in this alliance, and likely to lengthen the war. The Church would most prefer to see a coalition of the Western Powers with Germany; as a minimum, it wants a strong and united Germany as a barrier against Soviet Russia. The

Curia is putting aside its Italian sentiments. It senses that everything is at stake.[8]

The Holy See was equally concerned about the Communist threat to Rome itself. On October 14, the Cardinal Secretary of State spoke of it to Weizsäcker:

¶ Cardinal Maglione raised with me today the question of the danger which will threaten the Roman clergy in the event that possession of Rome passes from the hands of the German forces to the British and the city administration and police break down.[9]

It was in this atmosphere that German action against the Jews of Rome began.

[8] Telegram from Weizsäcker to Berlin, Oct. 7, 1943, ibid. (MS).
[9] Telegram from Weizsäcker to Berlin, Oct. 14, 1943, ibid. (MS).

Chapter VIII

THE DEPORTATION OF THE
ROMAN AND ITALIAN JEWS

October–December 1943

B EFORE DEALING with the events that marked the deportation of the Jews from Rome and Italy, I feel obliged to
examine very briefly the theory alleging fear on the part of the
Pope that if he raised any protest against the German anti-
Jewish measures, the Germans would take action against the
Vatican. It may, by the way, be suggested a priori that fear of
such an eventuality did not influence Pius XII's silence since
he persisted in that silence when the deportation of the Jews
from Hungary began in June 1944, at a time, that is, when
Rome and the Vatican were already under the protection of
Allied troops. Nevertheless, I shall give a short account of
the facts (and, incidentally, the intentions of the Germans) as
they could have been known to the Vatican in October 1943;
I shall do so by way of answer to the contention that between
October 1943 and June 1944 the reasons for silence on the
part of the Pope may have changed.

1. The Germans and Vatican City

IN CERTAIN BOOKS of memoirs written since World War II, mention is made of German plans to abduct the Pope. It is difficult to know whether the Nazis devised a plan of this nature, because there is no reference to it in any document. Indeed, the Wilhelmstrasse documents covering the autumn of 1943 seem to suggest the opposite. Before we look into them, let us recall Hitler's famous diatribe of July 26, 1943, against the Vatican.

Hitler had just learned of Mussolini's fate, and he was in a highly excited state. The occupation of Rome by airborne troops was under consideration. Thereupon, Hewel, Ribbentrop's representative at the Führer's headquarters, asked:

¶ "Shouldn't we say that the Vatican exits are to be occupied?" "That doesn't matter," answered Hitler, "I'm going into the Vatican right now. Do you think the Vatican bothers me? We'll grab it at once. First of all, the whole diplomatic corps is in there. I couldn't care less. That bunch is in there, we'll drag them out, the whole swinish pack of them . . . What of it? . . . We can apologize afterwards, that's nothing to worry about . . ."[1]

Thus Hitler, in a moment of extreme agitation, saw himself enter the Vatican, "drag out" the foreign diplomats who had schemed Mussolini's downfall and . . . withdraw, with apologies. Even under the shock of Mussolini's arrest, Hitler did not talk of occupying the Vatican, even less of taking action against the clergy or the Pope. In any case, all this was

[1] Helmut Heiber, ed.: *Hitlers Lagebesprechungen* (Stuttgart: Deutsche Verlags-Anstalt: 1962), p. 329.

nothing more than a reaction to the events of the moment. By September, when Italy had capitulated and the Germans entered Rome, their attitude was very different.

On September 10, when sporadic fighting was still going on in the streets of the Italian capital, Weizsäcker informed Berlin that Cardinal Maglione had again requested him to see that the Vatican City and its subsidiary establishments were respected by the forces of the Reich. Weizsäcker's dispatch added that normal communication between himself and the commander of the German troops had been interrupted.[2] A few hours later, communication was restored.

On the 17th, Ribbentrop asked Weizsäcker whether it was true, as indicated by an agency message, that the Pope had refused to receive a representative of Field Marshal Kesselring, commander of the German forces in Italy.[3] Next day, the Ambassador set the record straight: Kesselring had never asked for an audience with the Pope, nor had he asked that one of his envoys be received by the Sovereign Pontiff.[4] Two days later, the representative of the Reich wrote:

¶ The German occupation of Rome does not diminish the sovereignty of the Vatican. The Vatican transmitter has not been occupied by us because it stands inside Vatican City. The Pope is not hampered in his apostolic duties by German action. He is not our prisoner. No Italian is being denied access to St. Peter's. On the contrary, the Curia has been shown every consideration.

[2] Telegram from Weizsäcker to Berlin, Feb. 10, 1943, StS: V, AA, Bonn (MS).
[3] Telegram from Sonnleithner to Weizsäcker, Sept. 17, 1943, ibid., (MS).
[4] Telegram from Weizsäcker to Ribbentrop, Sept. 18, 1943, ibid., (MS).

Naturally, it would have been greatly welcomed by the Curia if the storm of war around Rome had receded, leaving the city untouched. The occupation of Rome by German troops is burdensome to the Vatican. In the early days of the occupation, when numerous vehicles were requisitioned here by the military, the Embassy had to take care that Vatican cars were not affected. Traffic between Vatican City and the numerous extraterritorial Vatican exclaves within Rome, as well as the other offices of the Curia in the City, had to be ensured. While fighting was in progress here, the movement of supplies for the Pope and the inmates of Vatican City from the orchards and vegetable gardens at Castel Gandolfo was interrupted. Here, too, the Embassy intervened to put matters right. An inconvenience that actually still exists today is the interruption of mail and telegraphic communication between the Vatican and the Italian Bishops and the foreign stations with which the Vatican transmitter has no direct traffic. In co-operation with Minister Rahn, the Embassy is making efforts to ease the situation, so far as military exigencies permit.[5]

Meantime, Allied propaganda continued to exploit the presence of German soldiers at the gates of the Vatican. On October 1, Roosevelt declared that "the Allied march northwards aims at freeing Rome, the Vatican and the Pope, much in the manner of a crusade.[6] Ribbentrop decided to take counteraction. On October 4, he wired to Weizsäcker:

¶ Now that Roosevelt has picked up the contention that Pope is a prisoner and the Vatican sealed off, and has attempted at the same time to hold us responsible, as of now, for any

[5] Telegram from Weizsäcker to Ribbentrop, Sept. 22, 1943, ibid., (MS).
[6] *Keesing's Contemporary Archives,* London, p. 6035.

possible destruction to Rome and the Vatican area, it seems appropriate to make clear the German decision to respect the Vatican State in every way and to put the clarification in a form which can be used later, if necessary, as an effective response to enemy agitation.

I therefore request you to seek an audience with the Pope and to draw his attention in emphatic terms to the malicious campaign of our opponents.

In doing so, you may make the following oral statement: "As the Curia is aware, enemy propaganda has been endeavoring, by fabrications of all kinds, since the German troops moved into Rome, to represent the Vatican as the victim of German violence. The behavior of the German troops already has given the lie unequivocally to these assertions. Despite this, the calumnies of our opponents against Germany are continuing. Thus, for example, these have been taken up by the Chief of State of the United States. In the face of this, the Reich Government affirms that Germany respects the sovereignty and integrity of the Vatican State to the full and that members of the German Armed Forces in Rome are conducting themselves accordingly.

"The Reich Government would welcome it if the Curia, on its part, could publish an unambiguous account of the situation and so ensure dissemination of the truth. You may further inform the Pope that the Reich Government would be particularly gratified if this rectification could come from the Pope's own mouth."

Ribbentrop then authorized his Ambassador to hand the Cardinal Secretary of State the following declaration:

¶ . . . on the German side, it is reaffirmed that the sovereignty and territorial integrity of the Vatican will be respected and that the German troops in Rome will behave accordingly. It is further promised on the German side that everything possible will be done to ensure that Vatican City does not become involved in combat.[7]

On October 9, Weizsäcker was received in audience by the Pope. Pius XII began by expressing his satisfaction at the steps taken by the German Embassy in the several cases in which the interests of the Vatican had conflicted with the requirements of the German forces occupying Rome:

¶ The Pope was fully cognizant of the slanders which our opponents, and now Roosevelt himself, are spreading about our troops in Rome. The Pope therefore unhesitatingly agreed in principle with the statement which I made, as instructed. He reserved his position regarding the drafting of a Vatican statement and on the form in which it would be published. However, I did not get the impression that the Pope wishes to enter the public arena himself. As regards the formulation, the Pope said it would be most effective if the Curia linked its statement to the one I made today.

I replied that my instructions spoke of the Curia's taking steps "of its own accord" to ensure dissemination of the truth.

The Pope thought that this, too, would be possible, though less valuable. In that event, he said, only the past could be discussed, whereas, according to his idea, the German declaration, which could also be interpreted as a promise would point toward the future if linked to a Vatican statement, and would therefore be more important.

[7] Telegram from Ribbentrop to Weizsäcker, Oct. 7, 1943, ibid. (MS).

Weizsäcker replied that he would have to ask his government for instructions.[8]

It is not possible here to follow the course of the negotiations between the Holy See and the Germans concerning the most appropriate form for a declaration indicating that the forces of the Reich had not interfered with Vatican sovereignty and that, further, the Curia had received an assurance that this would continue to be the case in future. We should also bear in mind that, at the moment when the Vatican was receiving such assurances through diplomatic channels, it was obtaining others through various unofficial intermediaries in contact with the German command: Father Pfeiffer, Father Leiber and, in particular, Msgr. Ludwig Kaas, whose nephew was a German officer in Rome, as was also the son of von Gerlach, a friend of the Monsignor.[9]

As a result of all this negotiation, Vatican Radio broadcast the following communiqué on October 19, 1943:

¶ To put an end to unfounded rumors, especially abroad, regarding the conduct of German troops towards the Vatican City, the German Ambassador to the Holy See, on behalf of his Government, has declared that Germany, in accordance with her policy so far of respecting the offices and integrity of the Roman Curia, as well as the sovereign rights of the Vatican City, is resolved to respect them in future. The Holy See, in acknowledging that the German troops have respected the Roman Curia and the Vatican City, has taken note of this assurance.[1]

It is therefore reasonable to suggest that in October

---

[8] Telegram from Weizsäcker to Ribbentrop, Oct. 8, 1943, ibid. (MS).
[9] *Journal de Genève*, July 27, 1964, doc. cit.
[1] *Keesing's Contemporary Archives*, London, 1943, p. 6166.

1943 the Holy See did not seem to fear German action against the Vatican, and even less against the person of the Sovereign Pontiff himself.[2]

2. *The Deportation of the Jews from Rome*

On October 6, Moellhausen, the German Consul in Rome, dispatched the following telegram, classified "Urgent, Most Secret" to Ribbentrop:

¶ Obersturmbannführer Kappler [of the Special Police] has been instructed by Berlin to seize the eight thousand Jews living in Rome and to take them to Upper Italy where they are to be liquidated. General Stahel, Town Commandant of Rome, informs me that he will permit this action only if it is in accordance with the wishes of the Reich Minister for Foreign Affairs. I personally am of opinion that it would be better business to draft the Jews, as in Tunis, for fortification work and shall put this view, in conjunction with Kappler, to General Field Marshal Kesselring.[3]

A day later, Moellhausen addressed a new telegram to Ribbentrop:

¶ Further to Telegram No. 192 of the 6th: General Field Marshal Albert Kesselring has asked Obersturmbannführer Kappler to defer planned action against the Jews for the time being. If steps should be taken nevertheless, he would

[2] American documents indicate that when the German forces entered Rome there were fears at the Holy See of Nazi action against the Vatican; but the correct conduct of the occupying forces soon reassured the Curia. Telegram from Tittmann to Hull, Oct. 25, 1943, *FRUS*, 1943, II, p. 951.

[3] Telegram from Moellhausen to Ribbentrop, Oct. 6, 1943, StS: Italien, AA, Bonn (MS).

prefer to have the able-bodied Jews of Rome drafted for fortification work.[4]

The reply from Berlin was not long delayed. On the 9th, Counselor of Legation Thadden wired Moellhausen:

¶ As directed by Führer's instruction, the 8,000 Jews living in Rome are to be taken to Mauthausen as hostages. Minister for Foreign Affairs requests you not to interfere in affair in any circumstances, but to leave it to the S.S.[5]

Why this hesitation on the part of Moellhausen, Stahel, and Kesselring? Was it a sudden access of pity? That is most unlikely. But it was known that many Jews had taken refuge in monasteries and churches, and it was feared that this time the Pope, as Bishop of Rome, would not be able to refrain from raising his voice. The psychological damage which such a protest might inflict on the German cause would be infinitely great. Was the extermination of 8,000 Jews worth this?

In Berlin, the belief probably was held that the Pope would not intervene. On the night of October 15 to 16, the operation began. 1259 Jews were seized; on October 18, 1007 were deported to Auschwitz.

For several days, the danger of an intervention by the Pope seemed real. On October 16, Msgr. Alois Hudal, rector of the German Church in Rome, sent the following letter to General Stahel:

¶ A high Vatican source in the immediate entourage of the Holy Father has just reported to me that the arrests of Jews

---

[4] Telegram from Moellhausen to Ribbentrop, Oct. 7, 1943, ibid., (MS).
[5] Telegram from Thadden to Moellhausen, Oct. 9, 1943, Inland II g: Juden in Italien, Bonn (MS).

of Italian nationality began this morning. In the interests of the good understanding existing hitherto between the Vatican and the High Command of the German Forces, which is primarily due to your Excellency's political farsightedness and magnanimity and will one day go down in the history of Rome, I earnestly request you to order the immediate cessation of these arrests in Rome and its environs. I fear that if this is not done the Pope will make a public stand against it, which could not fail to serve anti-German propaganda as a weapon against us Germans.[6]

The following day, Weizsäcker confirmed the information passed on by Msgr. Hudal:

¶ I can confirm the reaction of the Vatican to the removal of Jews from Rome, as given by Bishop Hudal (cf. Telegraphed Report from the Rahn Office of October 16). The Curia is dumbfounded, particularly as the action took place under the very windows of the Pope, as it were. The reaction could perhaps be muffled if the Jews were employed on work in Italy itself.

Circles hostile to us in Rome are turning the action to their own advantage to force the Vatican to drop its reserve. It is being said that in French cities, where similar things happened, the bishops took up a clear position. The Pope, as Supreme Head of the Church and Bishop of Rome, could not lag behind them. Comparisons are also being made between Pius XI, a much more impulsive person, and the present Pope.

Our opponents, in their propaganda abroad will certainly

6 Telegram from Gumpert to Berlin, Oct. 16, 1943, Inland II g: Juden in Italien, AA, Bonn (MS).

seize upon the present action in the same way in order to sow discord between us and the Curia.[7]

However, on October 28, Weizsäcker was able to announce to Berlin that the danger was past. The Pope would not protest:

¶ By all accounts, the Pope, although harassed from various quarters, has not allowed himself to be stampeded into making any demonstrative pronouncement against the removal of the Jews from Rome. Although he must count on the likelihood that this attitude will be held against him by our opponents and will be exploited by Protestant quarters in the Anglo-Saxon countries for purposes of anti-Catholic propaganda, he has done everything he could, even in this delicate matter, not to injure the relationship between the Vatican and the German Government or the German authorities in Rome. As there will presumably be no further German action to be taken in regard to the Jews here in Rome, this question, with its unpleasant possibilities for German-Vatican relations, may be considered as liquidated.

On the Vatican side, at any rate, there is one definite indication of this. *L'Osservatore Romano* of October 25/26 gives prominence to a semi-official communique on the Pope's loving-kindness which is written in the characteristically tortuous and obscure style of this Vatican paper, and says that the Pope lavishes his fatherly care on all people, regardless of nationality, religion *or race* [underlined in the text]. The manifold and increasing activity of Pius XII (it continues) has been intensified of late because of the augmented suffering of so many unfortunate people.

7 Telegram from Weizsäcker to Berlin, Oct. 17, 1943, Inland II A B: Juden in Italien, AA, Bonn (MS).

No objection can be raised to this public statement, the less so as its text, a translation of which is attached, will be understood by only very few people as having special reference to the Jewish question."[8]

Weizsäcker enclosed with his letter the text of the following article from *L'Osservatore Romano:*

L'Osservatore Romano, October 25/26, 1943, No. 250.

THE CHARITABLE ACTIVITY OF THE
HOLY FATHER

¶ Echoes of ever-increasing disaster caused by the prolongation of the present conflict are persistently reaching the Holy Father and exciting his compassion more than ever.

The Pope, having, as everyone knows, striven in vain to prevent the outbreak of war and having warned the leaders of the nations against resorting to the force of arms, which today is so frightful, has not shrunk from using all the means in his power to mitigate suffering of any kind arising out of this monstrous world holocaust.

With the accumulation of so much suffering, universal and paternal succor by the Pope has increased; it knows no bounds of nationality, religion *or race.*

This manifold and tireless activity on the part of Pius XII has been intensified still further of late by the heightened suffering of so many unfortunate people.

This was followed by an expression of hope for an early peace and a better world.

[8] Letter from Weizsäcker to Berlin, Oct. 28, 1943, ibid., (MS).

3. The Deportation of the Jews from Italy

GERMAN ACTION against the Jews was soon extended to the whole of Northern Italy, but with no great success. The majority of the 35,000 Jews living in that region succeeded in hiding; the local Italian authorities, both secular and religious, helped the Jews to find refuge. Then, on December 1, 1943, the Fascist Salo Republic promulgated a new law whereby all Jews in Italy were to be shut up in concentration camps and their property confiscated. The law, though it failed to achieve much effect, did, on this occasion, provoke a reaction from *L'Osservatore Romano*. Weizsäcker put his finger on the difference with great accuracy when he pointed out on December 3 that the Vatican, while refraining from all comment when measures were taken by the Germans, did express criticism when the authors (of such measures) were Italians.[9]

On December 3, Koester, the German Consul in Venice, reported the main points of a discussion which a friend of his had just had with the Cardinal Patriarch of that city:

¶ A personage who is a friend of mine has been received by the Patriarch for a discussion which has been reported to me in detail, evidently with the intention of having the information passed on by me to a higher level [wrote Koester].

The Patriarch pointed out that the Jewish question, as it was now being handled in Venice, was causing him grave concern. Last night, many arrests of poor, old and sick Jews were made in their homes by extreme Fascists, while wealthy and carefully screened Jews continued to move

[9] Telegram from Weizsäcker to Berlin, Dec. 3, 1943, ibid. (MS).

[209]

about freely in Venice, if they had not already fled from the city. This injustice was disturbing him so much that the only solution he could see would be for the measures against the Jews to be carried out by German authorities, because then justice would at least be guaranteed for all. It is well known that the Patriarch's chief wish is to have all Jews and half-Jews shut up in a ghetto. The Catholic Church (he said) could no longer stand by and watch such things without taking up a position against the present Italian Government which carried out these measures or at least tolerated them (*con questi procedimenti la chiesa sarà obligata a dichiararsi apertamente contro il governo fascista*).

The Patriarch emphasized further that Germany represented the only protection against Bolshevism as it moved ever closer, and to that extent Germany and the Vatican undoubtedly had common interests. Unfortunately, however, he was not in a position to come out into the open with a statement of this kind because many persons in leading positions in Germany were known to be pursuing pagan ideas (*idee pagane*), otherwise the Church would have no hesitation in declaring that Germany was the only power that could save Europe, and therefore the Vatican, from Bolshevism.

During the forty-five days of Badoglio's traitorous regime (he said), the Church had taken careful note that the real wirepullers were Masonic and Jewish circles, with the result that the situation was one of extreme jeopardy for the Church.

Last of all, the Patriarch repeated his opinion, shared in many other quarters here, that an administration in

German hands, combined with trustworthy Italian circles, would be the best solution.[1]

4. An Interview with the Pope on the Reich and the International Situation

ON DECEMBER 16, Kaltenbrunner, Chief of the Reich Security Police and Security Service, sent Ribbentrop a long report from one of his agents on "the attitude of the Pope regarding the international situation and the National-Socialist state." Here is the full text:

¶ A reliable local agent of proven worth, who is well known to the Pope from the time the Pope was Nuncio in Munich and Berlin, was in Rome from November 14 to 19, 1943, as a special courier of the [present] Nuncio and on instructions from Cardinal Bertram. In an hour-long conversation with the agent, the Pope made lengthy statements in which he defined his position in regard to the events of the day and on the subject of the relations between the Vatican and the German Reich. According to the agent's report, the Pope's attitude was as follows:

At the start, the discussion dealt with the bombing of the Vatican. The Pope said that although the investigation of this matter had not yet been concluded, he could not imagine that one of the belligerent powers could have had any part in it.[2]

He further made it absolutely clear that he had no in-

[1] Letter from Koester to Berlin of Dec. 7, 1943, Inland II A B: Juden in Italien, AA, Bonn (MS).
[2] On November 5, 1943, an unidentified aircraft had dropped several bombs on the Vatican City.

tention of leaving Rome and moving his residence to Northern Italy, let alone to another country.

Supplementing the remarks of the Pope on this matter, the agent stated that it was the general view in the Vatican that the bombing was staged by radical Fascist circles. It is also thought probable by many that the Fascists were supported by the S.S.

"Passing to the situation in Italy, the Pope then spoke of the rumors circulating in Germany to the effect that the Vatican had been informed in advance about the political events connected with the fall of the Mussolini Government and/or had participated actively in these or had played some other role. On this question, the agent was instructed by Cardinal Bertram to suggest that the Pope induce the Reich Government to issue an appropriate denial. The Pope protested most emphatically against any idea that he and the Holy See had been involved in any way, either actively or passively, in the fall of Mussolini and said that he, like every other Roman, had been taken completely by surprise by the events in Rome. It was quite true he had long had the impression that things could not go on as they were. He, too, had been thinking for some time of requesting the Reich Government to dissociate itself by a formal denial from the charges constantly being spread that he shared the responsibility to a greater or lesser degree for developments in Italy. The Pope further let it be understood that he was not at all in agreement with the Badoglio regime, particularly the refusal of the King to relinquish the throne.[3] He pointed out that the situation, particularly in Southern Italy, was continually sliding toward

---

[3] The Pope meant the Government in the southern portion of Italy which had been liberated by the Allies.

the Left and that, because of the King's refusal to abdicate, he was greatly concerned for the survival of the dynasty. He said in so many words:

"We note with great concern that in the new order of things in Southern Italy the influence of Freemasonry appears to be coming more and more to the fore, and that Communism is on the increase in a quite alarming manner, not only in Italy as a whole but also in Rome. Very menacing reports have come to Us from the South, but also from the industrial cities of Northern Italy (Bologna, Milan, Turin, and Genoa). We fear the worst if Germany should find herself obliged to evacuate these areas."

Bertram's instructions to the agent to request the Pope to give him an appreciation of the present situation and, if possible, a judgment on prospective developments elicited the following remarks:

In the face of the material superiority of the enemy powers, which was daily becoming more crushing, and in view of the increase in the number of fronts which was bound to occur, the war was already decided against Germany. In the next few weeks and months, military and political events would follow one another in rapid succession. Considering the attitude of the enemy powers toward National-Socialist Germany, he saw almost no hope for the conclusion of a peace which would be even partially tolerable for Germany. Ever since the beginning of the war, he had striven, far more than was publicly known, to restore peace. He was, he said, watching domestic developments in Germany with great anxiety. He believed that there, too, Communism was increasing strongly, and he regarded the 12½ million foreign workers as a very large element of danger.

In regard to the terror attacks [Allied bombardment], the Pope told the agent with impressive evidence of inward emotion:

"We empower you to state explicitly, to everyone, that the German people, in particular, have always been clasped in Our heart and that the German people, who are now being so sorely tried, are, more than any other nation, the object of Our very special concern. We have always given outward, as well as other, expression to our great sympathy for Germany, by interrupting Our private audiences so that members of the German Armed Forces who wished to visit Us might not have to wait unnecessarily.

"We make unceasing efforts to help, and especially to relieve the German people from the pressure of the dreadful terror attacks. Let everyone be convinced that, where the situation permits, we do everything that possibly can be done."

As has happened more than once with local agents, the Pope finally turned the conversation to the question of the danger of world Bolshevism and, in doing so, intimated yet again that at the present time National Socialism still represented the only bulwark against Bolshevism. He stated that though he was somewhat concerned about certain developments under National Socialism, the Church held out its hand in peace at all times, and especially now, in the interests of the nations; he added that the Church's basic inclination to get along with National Socialism had been demonstrated by the Concordat that had been signed. However, he had not so far gained the impression that there was an earnest wish and a firm intention on the other side to adopt a different attitude toward the Church. True, Weizsäcker, Germany's new representative at the Vatican, was personally very accommodating and he was visibly doing his utmost; indeed, of late, the Embassy had shown remarkable activity. Nevertheless, it was the Pope's impression that Weizsäcker had very little backing in Berlin and therefore could not achieve very much. "Moreover, incidents of the recent past—for example, the not very friendly attitude of official quarters toward the Catholic Church in the Tyrol—had shown that fundamentally there was, even today, very little willingness to arrive at an understanding. Nevertheless, all this could not, and would not, prevent him from grasping any hand that was held out to him in peace. The Church, he said, was an instrument of peace and reconciliation."

Finally, the Pope talked about Bolshevik religious policy and described the installation of the Patriarch Sergius merely as a very skillful move on the part of Stalin. All the same, this move had tied his (the Pope's) hands to an extraordinary extent and had put the Church in a rather difficult position vis-à-vis official Russia.

Further to the statements made above, it may be pointed out that another reliable local agent recently had a discussion with Archbishop Gröber of Freiburg, in the course of which Gröber made the following remarks about the present attitude of the Pope:

"At the present time, the Pope is engaged in an extremely hard battle with himself in regard to his attitude in the existing world situation and, in particular, toward National Socialism and Bolshevism. Even if it may be assumed that the regime in Russia will be forced to continue granting religious freedom, and that it will be possible, by dint of much sacrifice and hard work, to achieve successes for the Roman Catholic Church in Russia, these considerations are counterbalanced by the Pope's extremely deep distrust of Stalin's sincerity since it is impossible to believe a word he says.

"On the other hand, certain 'crimes' on the part of the Nazis (sterilization, euthanasia etc.) make it difficult for the Pope to effect a rapprochement with National Socialism. In spite of 'these crimes,' the Pope still hopes that, *in certain circumstances and if the necessity should arise for National Socialism in view of the present situation,* it may still be possible to reach a loyal relationship with the Reich and with National Socialism. All the same, it was his (Gröber's) personal opinion that the Pope's eyes must be opened and that he should be influenced not to allow himself to be duped by Hitler and the National Socialists."[3]

[3] Report by Kaltenbrunner to Ribbentrop, Dec. 16, 1943, Inland II g: Heiliger Stuhl, AA, Bonn (MS).

Chapter IX

THE DEPORTATION OF THE
HUNGARIAN JEWS
1944

GERMAN TROOPS occupied Hungary on March 19, 1944. On March 25, the Regent, von Horthy, appointed Sztojay, a henchman of the Germans, to head the new government. At the beginning of May, the deportation of the Jews began. In a report dated May 25, Counselor of Legation von Thadden described the steps already taken as well as future deportation plans:

¶ ... A survey showed that, up to noon on the 24th (of May), approximately 116,000 Jews had been shipped off to the Reich. Roughly 200,000 more have been concentrated and are waiting to be sent off. Concentration in the provinces north and northwest of Budapest will start on June 7. Around 250,000 Jews are expected ... It is believed that roughly 1,000,000 Jews (or perhaps a few more) will be rounded up ... The whole operation (including shipment) is to be completed about the end of July.[1]

---

[1] Report by von Thadden of May 25, 1944, Nuremberg Document NG 4089. There were 767,000 Jews in Hungary at the time. By the end of the war more than 500,000 had been exterminated.

In early June, events in the military sphere followed each other in swift succession. While the Russians were resuming their offensive in Poland and Romania, the Allies landed in Normandy, and on June 6 Rome was in their hands.

1. The Note from the Nuncio in Budapest and the Fears of the Wilhelmstrasse

On May 15, 1944, a few days after the deportations from Hungary began, the Apostolic Nuncio in Budapest, Msgr. Angelo Rotta, sent the following note to the Hungarian Ministry for Foreign Affairs:

¶ The Hungarian Government is preparing to deport 100,000 people. The whole world knows what this deportation in fact means.

The Office of the Apostolic Nuncio regards it as its duty to protest against such measures. Acting not out of a false sense of compassion but in the name of thousands of Christians, it requests the Hungarian Government once again not to continue its war against the Jews beyond the limits prescribed by the laws of nature and God's commandments, and to avoid any action against which the Holy See and the conscience of the entire Christian world would feel obliged to protest.[2]

The note sent by Nuncio Rotta is of particular importance because of the very fact that it was the first official protest against the deportation of Jews made by a representative of the Holy See.

The contents of the note were undoubtedly transmitted

[2] Hilberg, op. cit., p. 539.

to the Wilhelmstrasse, and its threat of public protests seems to have made the Germans uneasy for a while, as is indicated by an exchange of telegrams between Berlin and Veesenmayer, the Reich representative in Budapest.

On May 27, 1944, Schmidt, the Head of the Press Department in the German Foreign Office, addressed the following memorandum to Steengracht (transmitted to Veesenmayer):

¶ I learn from a very good review of operations against the Jews in Hungary, current and planned, that a large-scale operation against the Budapest Jews is envisaged for June.

The scope of the action planned will attract a great deal of attention abroad and is sure to touch off a violent reaction. Our enemies will raise an uproar, talk of manhunts and so on and will make use of atrocity reports to whip up feeling in their own countries and among the neutrals.[3]

Schmidt suggested that various measures be taken to create the impression that the Jews were saboteurs and were organizing military actions against the German forces.

Veesenmayer replied that he regarded such diversionary maneuvers as superfluous because, up to the moment when his telegram was written on June 8, 1944, there had been no public reaction abroad, although the measures envisaged against the Budapest Jews were plain for all to see. He wrote:

¶ So far as is known here, the evacuation measures carried out in Hungary up to now have not produced any major reaction abroad. No such reaction is likely to occur in the case of the operation against the Budapest Jews either, as it has been known for a long time that the ghettoization

---

[3] Memorandum from Schmidt to Steengracht, May 27, 1944, Nuremberg Document NG-2424.

process in Budapest, as elsewhere, is being pushed through to the end.[4]

2. *The Pastoral Letter of the Primate of Hungary*

DURING JUNE, the Jews of Budapest, aware of the fate awaiting them, circulated through the city some thousands of copies of an illicit handbill addressed to the Christians of Hungary, the text of which opened thus:

¶ To the Christians of Hungary:

In this final hour of their tragic destiny, the Jews of Hungary turn imploringly to the Christians of Hungary. They address their words to those whose existence they have shared for a thousand years, in good times and bad, on soil in which their ancestors are at rest.

We kept silent when we were robbed of our possessions, when we lost our human dignity, and our status as citizens. We did not decide upon this extreme step even when we were driven from our homes. But now our very lives are at stake. And this we write in pain: that the lives involved are those, alas, of but a fraction of Hungary's Jews . . .

In the name of our children, our aged, and our defenseless women, in the name of us all as we face certain death, a frightful death, we address this prayer to the Christian community of Hungary . . .[5]

Thereupon, on June 29, 1944, the Primate of Hungary, Msgr. Seredi, drew up and published this pastoral letter:

¶ We do not deny that many Jews have had a destructive and harmful influence on the economic, social and moral

[4] Telegram from Veesenmayer to Berlin, June 8, 1944, Nuremberg Document NG-2260.
[5] Document in Jenö Lévai: *Eichmann en Hongrie* (Budapest: Editions Pannonia; 1961), pp. 116 f.

life of Hungary. It is also true that the others did not protest against the actions of their coreligionists. We do not doubt that the Jewish question must be settled in a legal and just manner. Consequently, we have no objection to the measures taken, to the extent that they affect the financial system of the state. We do not protest either against the elimination of the noxious influence of the Jews. On the contrary, we wish it to disappear. But it would be neglect of our moral and episcopal duty if we did not raise a warning voice against any assault on justice, against suffering inflicted on our Hungarian compatriots and devout members of our Catholic Church, solely on account of their religion.

We have not been able to obtain the modifications we wished, namely, the cessation of illegal limitations on the rights of citizens and, particularly, an end to the deportations. However, because we had confidence in the Christian spirit and in the humanitarian sentiments of the members of the Government, we did not abandon all hope, in spite of the meager results we have obtained up to now. That is why we have made no public pronouncement, but have, in the meantime, done everything possible to attain our objective.

. . . Nevertheless, we note with great consternation that, in spite of our efforts, all negotiations on the most important points so far have proven almost completely ineffectual. We therefore solemnly reject all responsibility for the consequences . . . Pray and work for our Hungarian compatriots and particularly for our Catholic brethren, our Catholic Church and our beloved Hungary.[6]

6 Hilberg, op. cit., pp. 539 f.

3. *The Intervention of the Chief Rabbis*
of Palestine at the Holy See

THE WHOLE of the Jewish world watched in agony as events in Hungary unfolded.

Since 1943, the Executive Committee of the Jewish Agency in Palestine had been in close contact with Msgr. Angelo Giuseppe Roncalli, Apostolic Delegate of the Holy See at Istanbul and the future Pope John XXIII. Msgr. Roncalli spared no effort to succor the Jews of Central Europe and the Balkans; he seems even to have addressed words of encouragement to the Nuncios in the Balkan countries, as might be inferred from the note sent to him on March 25, 1944, by M. Haim Barlas, the Jewish Agency delegate in Istanbul:

¶ Your Excellency:

I was very much touched by your reception today and by the most humane sentiments toward our unhappy people which you are showing in these fateful moments. It caused me great satisfaction to learn that you will be kind enough to send a message by telegram to the Holy See and to the Apostolic Delegates at Bucharest and Budapest, asking them to use their influence in these matters along the lines we discussed. I have taken the liberty, Your Excellency, of bringing the above to the notice of the Executive of the Jewish Agency and of the Chief Rabbi, Dr. Herzog . . .[7]

[7] Note from M. Barlas to Msgr. Roncalli, March 25, 1944, Zionist Archives, Jerusalem, (MS). The Zionist Archives contain a large number of documents concerning the incessant activity of Nuncio Roncalli on behalf of the Jews. We should stress, however, that Msgr. Roncalli is reported to have stated that everything he did in this sphere was done at the instance of the Pope.

On May 22, 1944, the Chief Rabbis of Palestine, Rabbis Isaac Herzog and Ben-Zion Meir Uziel, sent, through the medium of the Apostolic Delegate's office in Cairo, a telegram to the Sovereign Pontiff, asking for his urgent intervention against the deportations from Hungary:

¶ Request you convey to Vatican unutterable anguish at terrible catastrophe now overtaking one and a half million Jews in Balkan countries especially Hungary where situation created identical with that in Poland for remnants of people of Israel in Nazi-occupied Europe stop we appeal to Your Holiness to use your great influence as earlier with Hungarian nation to prevent diabolical plan to exterminate its Jews stop May Your Holiness arouse secular and spiritual leaders under Cardinal Archbishop to make supreme effort to save Jews as a whole and particularly help them to leave Hungary stop May God bless Your Holiness and may we soon see fulfillment of prophecy earth shall be filled with knowledge of God as the ocean bed is covered with water Amen.

Herzog   Uziel, Chief Rabbis, Palestine.[8]

The transfer of Hungarian Jews to Auschwitz continued. From June 9 to July 9, 1944, more than 437,000 were deported.[9]

Protest messages poured into Budapest; among those protesting to the Regent were the King of Sweden and the President of the International Red Cross. On June 25, Pius XII himself sent the following message.

---

[8] Telegram from Herzog and Uziel to Pius XII, May 22, 1944, ibid., (MS)
[9] Hilberg, op. cit., p. 547.

¶ Supplications have been addressed to Us from different sources that we should exert all Our influence to shorten and mitigate the sufferings that have, for so long, been peacefully endured on account of their national or racial origin by a great number of unfortunate people belonging to this noble and chivalrous nation. In accordance with Our service of love, which embraces every human being, Our fatherly heart could not remain insensible to these urgent demands. For this reason we apply to Your Serene Highness, appealing to your noble feelings, in the full trust that Your Serene Highness will do everything in your power to save many unfortunate people from further pain and sorrow.[1]

The Nuncio, Msgr. Angelo Rotta, also displayed great activity.[2] At that point the Chief Rabbi of Palestine, Dr. Herzog, requested an audience with the Pope.

The efforts of Chief Rabbi Herzog to gain access to the Pope seemed to come up against a great deal of resistance on the part of the Vatican. In July 1944 Jacob Herzog, the Chief Rabbi's son and secretary, sent Isaac Ben-Zwi, a member of the Jewish Agency Executive (and a future President of the State of Israel) the following letter:

¶ I am writing to inform you, in accordance with your request, about the negotiations that have taken place with representatives of the Vatican and with the Vatican di-

---

[1] Eugene Levai: *The Black Book on the Martyrdom of Hungarian Jewry*, edited by Lawrence P. Davis (Zurich: Central European Times Publishing Co.; 1948), p. 232.
[2] For details, see "Pope Pius XII and the Jews of Hungary in 1944," the text of a lecture delivered by the Reverend Father Robert A. Graham before the United States Catholic Historical Society on May 7, 1964.

rectly, with the object of obtaining an audience with the Pope for the Chief Rabbis (Herzog and Uziel).

1) On 2 Tammuz (July) I had a talk with the secretary to the Apostolic Delegation in Jerusalem and acquainted him with the wish of the Chief Rabbis to go to Rome for this purpose. I told him of the latest information from Hungary and of the wish, indeed the urgent plea of the Chief Rabbis to be received by the Pope so that they could express to him the anguish of the entire Jewish people and decide what concrete measures could be taken to save them. The secretary immediately had our message passed to the representative of the Vatican in Cairo for onward transmission to the Vatican.

2) On 8 Tammuz, the Governing Board of the Jewish Agency informed us that the Rescue Committee had made a positive decision concerning the journey of the Chief Rabbis. On the 9th, I had another meeting with the secretary to the Vatican Delegation and explained to him the urgency of this journey; he wired to Cairo once more to inquire about developments.

3) On 11 Tammuz, the Chief Rabbis sent a telegram to Archbishop Spellman in New York informing him of the request they had made to the Vatican and asking him to come to Rome himself to discuss measures for saving the Jews. The same day, Chief Rabbi Herzog telegraphed to the Cardinal of Ireland, asking him if he would intervene to hasten arrangements for the audience which had been requested. Until today, no reply to either of these telegrams has been received.

4) On 15 Tammuz, the secretary to the Vatican Delegation telephoned to inform me that he had received a telegram from Cairo to the effect that the Vatican Dele-

gate had left for Rome on urgent business; before his departure he had left instructions for the Chief Rabbi to be informed that he himself would present at the Vatican the request of the Chief Rabbis for an audience. The secretary told me that he imagined the Delegate would arrive in Rome on the 16th. He himself was leaving for Cairo and promised to advise me as soon as he received information from Rome.

5) That day, the Chief Rabbis telegraphed to the Secretary of State in the Vatican, notifying him that the Palestine Delegate would submit their request to him in the course of the next few days. They asked the Secretary of State, in view of the latest information, to do all he could to hasten matters.

6) On 23 Tammuz, we sent a wire to the secretary to the Vatican Delegation, who is still in Cairo, telling him of our astonishment at having as yet received no reply to our request and asking him to send the Vatican a reminder.[3]

On September 5, 1944, the Chief Rabbi was invited to Cairo to meet Msgr. Hughes, the Papal Delegate to Egypt and Palestine. The record of their meeting is reproduced below in extenso:

¶ *Chief Rabbi:* I received the telegram informing me of your arrival in Cairo and I hurried to see you.

Msgr. Hughes: I am very happy to receive you, Your Reverence, and I have an important special message for you.

Chief Rabbi: Your Eminence is aware that the British Foreign Office has expressed willingness to handle the tech-

[3] Letter from J. Herzog to Ben-Zwi, July 1944, Zionist Archives, Jerusalem (MS).

nical problems involved in my journey to the Vatican. I did not leave for the Vatican because I had received a telegram from Cardinal Maglione, the Secretary of State (whose passing I deplore), which ran as follows: "Reference your proposed journey to Rome, Msgr. Hughes will soon return (from Rome) with a definite answer. I would inform you that Msgr. Hughes has devoted active and special attention to all the problems which Your Reverence brought to the Holy Father's notice. Steps have been taken, as a result of which the general situation has improved. Msgr. Hughes will shortly return and give Your Reverence a full explanation."

Msgr. Hughes: On my arrival in Rome, I conveyed Your Reverence's request to visit the Vatican to the Holy Father in person and to the Secretary of State's Office, as I had promised. In the consultations that followed, Cardinal Maglione, who recalled having met Your Reverence during the first year of the war, exerted considerable influence. Afterward, I drafted a telegram inviting Your Reverence to come. I took it to be cleared, but it was held back at the last moment. The reason was the Holy Father's fear that Your Reverence's coming to the Vatican in connection with measures to save the people of Israel might, perhaps, drive the Germans to wreak vengeance on the remnants of Jewry in Europe. I went to visit the Holy Father in the company of Mr. J. A. Clifford, the British Minister who is Britain's delegate responsible for dealing with refugee matters in Italy. On this point, I may tell Your Reverence that the Minister is a veritable saint; he is working day and night to save the Jewish people; he has detailed information on what is happening in the occupied territories and he can often be seen at the Secretary of State's Office with rescue plans. The destruction of European Jewry has changed him from the cheerful person he was into a man weighed down with anguish, and his face now never shows a smile. I must tell you, Your Reverence, that in the course of the interview a strange expression passed over the Holy Father's face, an expression of extreme suffering, the like of which I have never seen before. The Holy Father said: "We must do all in our power to save the people of Israel. But every step we take must be calculated with the greatest caution, because I could not bear the idea that our activity might have an effect opposite to the one intended and cause the death of still more Jews. The Holy Father particularly asked me to meet Your Reverence and to give you a full explanation. Your Reverence knows that nothing is further from the truth than the hypothesis that the Holy Father would not wish to meet you. Mr. Clifford, the British Minister, shares the Holy Father's opinion.

Chief Rabbi: I thank the Pope; I understand his point of view very well and I accept it. Please tell me what you have to say on the subject of the situation itself.

Msgr. Hughes: When we were informed that the deportations from Hungary had begun, the Holy Father made approaches to the Hungarian Government. I do not possess all the details of the negotiations between the Hungarian Government and ourselves, but I can tell your Reverence that the matter was prepared by the Holy Father himself, with all his wisdom and understanding of diplomacy. We rejoiced to learn that the deportations had ceased. I can inform Your Reverence about the situation in Italy, where many Jews have been saved by the Church.

When the Germans took control of the country, orders were given to all monasteries to conceal Jews. In Rome, for example, my brothers, the White Friars, have a monastery which houses four priests; we kept thirty-two Jews hidden in that monastery for a whole year. It was an act of Providence that the monastery was not searched because it is unlikely that the German Intelligence Service did not realize that for a year food for thirty-six people was delivered to a place which was supposed to be inhabited by four. In the convent of the English Church, dozens of Jews had been hidden. One day, some German officers arrived and demanded that the Jews be handed over to them. The Mother Superior refused, declaring that the convent was under the personal protection of the Holy Father and that no one could enter it without his authority. To her great astonishment, the Germans withdrew, had some discussion outside for a few moments and left for good. But in another convent, an Irish convent, the Germans insisted on making a search. The building had only one door, and when the Germans crossed the threshold, dozens of Jews concealed on the upper floor were seized with fear. A German priest saved the situation by confusing the soldiers as he led them from room to room, and thus got them out of the house without incident. One could go on relating deeds of this kind in great number. The Germans had a complete list of the priests who had organized help for the Jews. All those priests were hidden in the Vatican precincts and did not emerge until Rome was taken by the Allies. Your Honor certainly knows that a great many Jews were concealed inside the Vatican itself and particularly at Castel Gandolfo, where the Holy Father spends his holidays. The Germans took their revenge in Northern Italy by executing several priests who had helped to save the Jews. The atrocities committed by the Germans are beyond imagination, and I was able to grasp the meaning of the information given to me by the British Minister about the death chambers in Poland when I myself visited the torture chamber in Rome into which Jews were cast purely because they were Jews. Many non-Jews were also thrown in there because they were anti-Nazi. The terrible thing is that defeat does not make the Germans put a stop to their atrocities, even when they know that this will cost them dear, and that is why the Holy Father demands the greatest caution in rescue operations.

Chief Rabbi: I thank the Pope and the Church with all my heart for the help they have given, and I should like to know if you have any news from other countries.

Msgr. Hughes: I have concerned myself mainly with the Hungarian problem, but I can tell you very confidentially, Your Reverence, that many German priests whom the Holy Father wished to appoint as Bishops did not receive the approval of the German authorities because they had opposed the atrocities. The Nuncio at Kovno was compelled by the Germans to leave because of his forcefulness in opposing the extermination of the Jews. At the Vatican, there are complete files covering the whole situation and dealing with the considerable amount of work that has been done to save the people of Israel. I do not have all the details, but when Your Reverence visits the Vatican they will show you all the documents.

Chief Rabbi: I should like to offer you a few suggestions concerning the remnants of Hungarian Jewry. Our information is that the deportations are continuing, although on a less extensive scale than before. The escape routes, on the other hand, have been closed and the fact is that the only means that now exists of saving the Jews is through influence from within which might bring the atrocities to a halt. The Pope would be the most important person who could exert that influence. I suggest, then, that the Pope make a public appeal to the Hungarian people and call upon them to place obstacles in the way of the deportation; that he declare in public that any person obstructing the deportation will receive the blessing of the Church, whereas any person aiding the Germans will be denounced.

Msgr. Hughes: I shall convey your Reverence's suggestion to the Holy Father. I believe the Holy Father will fear that a public appeal to the Hungarian people may drive the Germans to liquidate the rest of the Hungarian Jews. The Germans still have sufficient strength in Hungary to do that, even against the will of the Hungarians. According to our knowledge, a large part of Hungary will be included in the inner redoubt which the Germans will defend to the last.

Chief Rabbi: I understand your argument. But if the Pope considers my suggestion feasible, I should be grateful to him to keep it in mind. The moment may come when an appeal of this kind will be useful and when there will no longer be any danger of vengeance.

Msgr. Hughes: Your Reverence is right in that and I shall pass on the suggestion.

Chief Rabbi: This morning, we received a telegram from Switzerland stating that the Governments of Sweden and Switzerland have approached the Hungarian Government with a demand that the deportations shall not be resumed. There certainly must have been a similar intervention on the part of the Pope.

Msgr. Hughes: Your Reverence may be absolutely sure that the Holy Father is doing all that it is possible to do but does not like publicity. He intervenes when and where intervention is most favorable.

Chief Rabbi: I should further like to ask for an intervention by the Pope in Slovakia, where certain members of the government are Catholics and where there are still thousands of Jews.

(Msgr. Hughes wrote down the request.) The Chief Rabbi then made the same request in connection with the Jews in Poland and other countries and suggested that in Hungary, and in the other countries, the Pope issue an order that Jews be concealed, similar to that given in Italy. [It is known that Jews were being hidden by the Church in Slovakia.]

¶ *Msgr. Hughes:* Has Your Reverence any other suggestions to make?

Chief Rabbi: With your permission, I shall ask my son if he has anything to suggest. [The Chief Rabbi's son was also his secretary.]

J. D. Herzog: You mentioned that in Rome some Jews in a convent were saved as the result of a statement by the Mother Superior that the convent had been placed under the personal protection of the Pope. Would it not be possible to use the same argument in places where Jews have been hidden, or will be hidden, in Hungary or elsewhere? Could one not go further and notify the Hungarian Government that the Pope had extended his personal protection to the camps where Jews are concentrated? Surely it would be possible to find a diplomatic channel for doing this.

Msgr. Hughes: That is a suggestion that deserves our full attention and I shall transmit it to Rome at once, al-

[232]

though priests so far have been forbidden to enter camps where Jews are held; nevertheless, it is a very important suggestion.

Chief Rabbi: If Hungarian Bishops were to go into the camps and announce publicly that, if deportation of Jews went on, they (the Bishops) would go and die with them, I think it would be difficult for the Germans to continue the deportations.

Msgr. Hughes: The Bishops in France and other countries have carried out demonstrations of that kind. When the Germans began deporting the Jews, they (the Bishops) went into the streets wearing a yellow star. This action made a considerable impression and, in some places, rendered deportation impossible. But Your Honor will understand that realization of your proposal would require "unity of action."

At the end of the interview, the Chief Rabbi asked that the thanks of the people of Israel be conveyed to the Pope, together with the Chief Rabbi's hope that the Holy Father would not relax his efforts to save the Jewish people. The Chief Rabbi added that the activities of the Catholic Church aimed at saving the people of Israel would heighten the radiance cast by religion throughout the world, and he expressed the wish that when he paid a visit to the Vatican, he would be supplied with all the details so that they could be written into the history of the people of Israel.

On Sunday morning, August 10, the Chief Rabbi sent the following letter to Msgr. Hughes, who was about to depart for Rome:

¶ I am leaving Cairo this morning and I wish to thank you again for the help you have given and are giving in a most sacred cause: the saving of the remnants of our tortured people. I would ask you at the same time to beg his Holiness to intervene with the Allies on their behalf. If His Holiness the Pope could also make the representatives of the German Government understand that continued torture of the survivors of the Jewish people would render it more and more difficult for civilized humanity to make any kind of a gesture toward them, this might, perhaps, prevent them from entirely destroying those who have escaped persecution. I am convinced that the Pope will understand the usefulness of this suggestion and will act in this sense.

In these critical moments, the eyes of the people of Israel, and of all humanity longing for liberty, are turned on the Pope. All our suggestions are in his hands, so that he may, in his wisdom, make use of them at a time and in a manner that seem to him most opportune. We believe with certainty that the Pope will not remain indifferent to the greatest tragedy that history has ever known. May God guide his steps.

Please inform me immediately of any reply from the Vatican.[4]

Certain of the explanations given by Msgr. Hughes were correct. It was true, for example, that at the time when the Apostolic Delegate was having discussions with Chief Rabbi Herzog, the deportations from Hungary temporarily ceased. At the beginning of July 1944, after fresh successes by the Russian troops, Regent Horthy ordered Sztojay to prevent the transfer of Jews left in Budapest to the Reich or to Poland. The deportations were resumed in October, after the Germans had forced Horthy to resign, had removed him to

---

[4] Undated, unsigned memorandum, Zionist Archives, Jerusalem (MS).

Germany and formed a government made up of Hungarian National Socialists (the Arrow Cross), with Szálasi as Premier.

Other parts of Msgr. Hughes's statements, on the other hand, are more difficult to interpret. Thus, the Apostolic Delegate cited the example of French Bishops who, in protest against the deportations, had gone into the streets wearing a yellow star and, by so doing, had succeeded in preventing the shipment of Jews to the East. Now there never was such a demonstration by French Bishops, as Msgr. Hughes must have known. The Chief Rabbi for his part, had no means of judging whether or not these details were true. By the same token, the statements of the Apostolic Delegate with regard to the many German clergymen who were alleged to have opposed Hitler were, to say the least, exaggerated.

However, what strikes one most in reading this interview is the way Msgr. Hughes dwelt on the particular cases in which Jews in Italy were saved, which he related in circumstantial detail; whereas, though promising to submit the matter to the Pope, he tried to head off any concrete proposals from the Chief Rabbi for a rescue operation on a broader scale.

Judging from the documents known to us, the Holy See does not seem to have paid any heed to the concrete proposals put forward by the Chief Rabbi of Palestine.

CONCLUSION

AT THE END of this study, which claims to be nothing more than an analysis of documents, I cannot make any definite answer to the questions raised by the wartime policies of the Holy See toward the Third Reich because I have only incomplete documents at my disposal.

I must content myself with pointing out that on two important points the German documents show impressive agreement: on the one hand, the Sovereign Pontiff seems to have had a predilection for Germany which does not appear to have been diminished by the nature of the Nazi regime and which was not disavowed up to 1944; on the other hand, Pius XII feared a Bolshevization of Europe more than anything else and hoped, it seems, that Hitler Germany, if it were eventually reconciled with the Western Allies, would become the essential rampart against any advance by the Soviet Union toward the West.

Setting out from these two elements of knowledge, which are powerfully bolstered by the German documents, one can pose certain questions relating to the Pope's silence in the face of the extermination of the Jews. With the documentation in its present state, the replies cannot be other than hypothetical. Consequently, lacking the irrefutable testimony of any document, I shall refrain from establishing a link between the two assertions just made and the silence of the Holy See.

Conclusion

Let us simply recall that, *according to the documents,* we have at our disposal four explanations, given either by the Sovereign Pontiff or by his Secretary of State, concerning that silence.

According to Cardinal Maglione, the Sovereign Pontiff could not condemn specific atrocities, while Pius XII pointed out that he could not condemn the German atrocities without condemning the Bolshevik atrocities.

In his letter to Msgr. Preysing, the Sovereign Pontiff wrote that it was to avoid still greater evils that he was not abandoning his restraint.

Lastly, in his address to the Sacred College in June 1943, Pius XII took up the same argument and added another reason (less clearly expressed) for keeping silent: the futility of all the approaches already made to the Germans.

It may further be noted that the Wilhelmstrasse archives which I have been able to consult contain no record of any démarche made by the Holy See to the Germans on the subject of the Jews, with the exception of the three interventions undertaken by Msgr. Orsenigo, whose nature I have indicated. However, as I have already emphasized, it is possible that Vatican interventions did take place and that the German accounts have disappeared.

Finally, a reading of the German documents raises, ineluctably, two questions:

How is it conceivable that at the end of 1943 the Pope and the highest dignitaries of the Church were still wishing for victorious resistance by the Nazis in the East and therefore seemingly accepted by implication the maintenance, however temporary, of the entire Nazi extermination machine?

How can one explain the manifestations of special pre-

[237]

dilection which the Pope continued to lavish on the Germans, even in 1943, when he was aware of the nature of the Hitler regime?

The historian, while noting the lacunae, is reduced to the hope that the essential documents he lacks, and particularly the documents of the Vatican archives, soon will be published so that the events and personages can be brought into proper perspective.

INDEX

[i]

SAUL FRIEDLÄNDER was born in Prague in 1932. In 1939 the family was forced to flee to France where, in 1942, his parents were taken by the Nazis, deported, and killed in Auschwitz. The child was hidden in a Catholic monastery until the end of the war. He came to Israel in 1948, and has been an Israeli citizen since that date. After service in the Israeli Army Mr. Friedländer attended the School of Law and Economics in Tel-Aviv (1950–3). He attended the Institut d'études politiques in Paris (1953–5), and was its highest-ranking graduate. From 1956 to 1961 he served as Secretary to the President of the World Zionist Organization, and as Head of the Scientific Department of Israel's Ministry of Defense. Mr. Friedländer earned his Ph.D. in Political Science in two years at the Graduate Institute of International Studies in Geneva, where he is now an Associate Professor of Contemporary History. His book, *Hitler and the United States, 1939–1941,* was published in French in 1963, in German in 1965, and an American edition is planned for 1966. *Pius XII and the Third Reich* has been published so far in French, German, Dutch, Italian, Spanish, and English. Its author resides with his wife and two sons in Geneva, Switzerland.

A NOTE ON THE TYPE

THE TEXT of this book was set on the Linotype in a face called TIMES ROMAN, designed by Stanley Morison for The Times (London), and first introduced by that newspaper in 1932.

Among typographers and designers of the twentieth century, Stanley Morison has been a strong forming influence, as typographical advisor to the English Monotype Corporation, as a director of two distinguished English publishing houses, and as a writer of sensibility, erudition, and keen practical sense.

Composed, printed, and bound by
The Haddon Craftsmen, Inc., Scranton, Pa.
Typography and binding design by
WARREN CHAPPELL

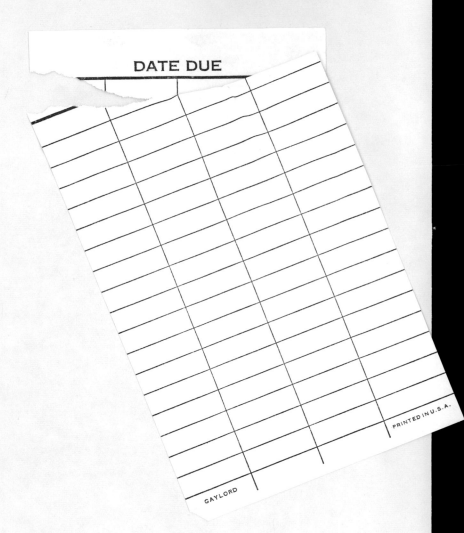

DATE DUE

PRINTED IN U.S.A.

GAYLORD